THE DESERT LAKE
The Story of Nevada's Pyramid Lake

THE
DESERT LAKE

The Story of Nevada's Pyramid Lake

By

SESSIONS S. WHEELER

ILLUSTRATED WITH PHOTOGRAPHS

The CAXTON PRINTERS, Ltd.
CALDWELL, IDAHO
1987

◁ PYRAMID LAKE

First printing December, 1967
Second printing February, 1968
Third printing February, 1969
Fourth printing July, 1974
Fifth printing June, 1980
Sixth printing September, 1987

Standard Book Number 87004-139-8
Library of Congress Catalog Card No. 87-70407

Lithographed and bound in the United States of America by
The CAXTON PRINTERS, Ltd.
Caldwell, Idaho 83605
148209

To a Fishing Partner
JIM CURRAN
Remembering an evening when
the big ones were feeding
on the surface of the
Desert Lake

Acknowledgments

IN ATTEMPTING to record the story of Pyramid Lake, the writer received the cooperation of many interested Nevadans. To assure accuracy, sections of the manuscript were submitted to authorities in particular fields, and, in this regard, I am especially indebted to Thomas J. Trelease, Chief of Fisheries of the Nevada State Fish and Game Commission, and to Donald R. Tuohy, Curator of Archaeology of the Nevada State Museum.

Mrs. Maude Heller, of the Fish Springs Ranch; Mr. Verne Whittey, of Reno; and Mr. Fred Crosby, of Sutcliffe, provided information which aided in salvaging part of the lake's history. Thomas C. Wilson furnished important map and other information, including Frémont's probable route in 1844. Other technical assistance was received from H. Claude Dukes, Federal Court Watermaster; Don Clendenon, United States Geological Survey; H. S. Richards and B. L. Harris, United States Bureau of Reclamation; Ira LaRivers, Donald Cooney, and James Firby, University of Nevada; Fred Wright and Kay Johnson, Nevada Fish and Game Commission; Mrs. Kay Fowler and Dr. Richard Licata, Desert Research Institute; Paul Gemmill, Nevada Mining Association; Ira Lutsey, Nevada Bureau of Mines; George Hardman,

Nevada Department of Conservation and Natural Resources; W. Verne Woodbury, biologist; and M. D. Mifflin, Desert Research Institute; and R. B. Morrison, United States Geological Survey.

Photographs or other aids were provided by Adrian F. Atwater, Mrs. Clara Beatty, Donald L. Bowers, Robert Cowles, James Calhoun, Art Champagne, Allen Crosby, Harry and Joan Drackert, William Daniel, Robert Hall, Dan Hellman, Mrs. Inez Johnson (Cover Photograph), Frank Johnson, Don King, Frank Leonard, John Sanford, Simon Simonean, Robert Leland, Phillip Ternan, Mrs. Margaret Wheat, Thomas R. C. Wilson, II, Miss Linda Loeffler and the expert photographers of the University of Nevada Audio-Visual Department, Mrs. Margaret Shaw, and Sol Savitt.

Robert D. Armstrong, Dr. Helen Poulton, and Mrs. Shirley Smith of the University of Nevada Library; Mrs. Alene DeRuff; Dr. Effie Mona Mack, Nevada historian; and personnel of the Washoe County Library were very helpful in regard to reference research.

I wish to mention my efficient typist and niece, Gaylene Henderson, who, regardless of her own responsibilities, was always willing to type each completed section of her Uncle Buck's manuscript, and to thank Tom Little for his criticisms and aid in proofreading.

And finally my gratitude to Mrs. Margaret Pead of Caxton for her experienced advice on the story of the desert lake.

Contents

List of Illustrations

Page

THE DESERT LAKE
The Story of Nevada's Pyramid Lake

CHAPTER I

Prehistory

APPROXIMATELY four thousand years would pass before the Egyptian King Khufu would build his great pyramid, and the teachings of Christianity were more than seven thousand years distant when a man stood on a ledge above the shore of a desert lake.

To this man, the Earth seemed very old. While winter winds had howled outside his cave, he had listened to the stories of his people—the legends, passed down through the centuries, of the hunters who had crossed the great land bridge of the North and entered a new world. Over infinite time others had followed, gradually moving southward from a country of snow and ice into a land bountiful in game and the other necessities for life. The legends told that when the ocean rose again to cover the great bridge between two continents, his people had continued to come to the new land, spanning the water barrier by paddling skin boats or crossing on the winter ice.

Always farther, the hunters of the mammoth and the others had pushed southward, passing bands of their people who, content with the area they had occupied, were living in harmony with their environment.

The man on the ledge paused in his work of removing a broken stone spearpoint from its shaft to watch a fish glide through the water below him. His ancestors had stopped at this desert lake, so the old stories claimed, because of the fish and other food it offered. When they had come to it, many generations ago, the lake had been so large that a man could not travel around it between one winter and the next. But through the centuries that followed, there were many years when only small amounts of rain and snow fell on the tall mountains to the west, and gradually the lake shrank. Now there were smaller lakes—puddles, the stories called them—of the great lake. One was over the mountains to the east; another was to the south.

The sinew which bound the sharpened stone to its shaft was now loose, and the damaged point dropped to the ledge, slipping into a shallow fissure in the tufa-encrusted rock.

A new spearhead was fastened into place, and the man began climbing down toward the shore of the lake which would provide his next meal. He hesitated once, at the base of the ledge, to consider if he should retrieve and resharpen the broken point. But it was a steep climb back, and he was hungry, and he decided against it.

And so a fragment of flaked black stone, wedged in a crevice above a desert lake, remained undisturbed for another man to see—nine thousand years later.

The parent of the desert lake probably was born approximately seventy thousand years ago, in the latter part of the Pleistocene epoch of our geologic calendar. During the following sixty thousand years, while the last great ice sheet from the North crept down and then retreated from what is now north-central and northeastern United States, relatively small glaciers periodically formed and melted in the Sierra Nevada and other mountains of the West. Over the thousands of years the climate changed many times, and the parent lake, Lahontan, responded to these changes, its fluctuations synchronized to the size of the glaciers in the nearby mountains. When the climate was cooler and wetter, the glaciers were extensive and the lake was high, several times covering an area of more than eight thousand square miles of what is now northwestern Nevada and northeastern California. When warmer and drier periods settled over the Great Basin, desiccation of the great lake occurred, and geologists believe that it may have dried up completely over at least one long period. During most of the last eight to nine thousand years, the lake probably has remained at relatively low levels. And during its low-level stages, the deepest of its "puddles" was the desert lake, Pyramid.

That men lived in caves along the desert lake's shore as long as eleven thousand years ago seems quite certain. Deep layers of dry dust within the caves have recently yielded preserved organic material associated with human occupancy which radioactive carbon measurements have dated more than eleven thousand years before the present. It is possible that future archaeological exploration may move this date thousands of years farther back into antiquity.

Anthropologists generally agree that these first

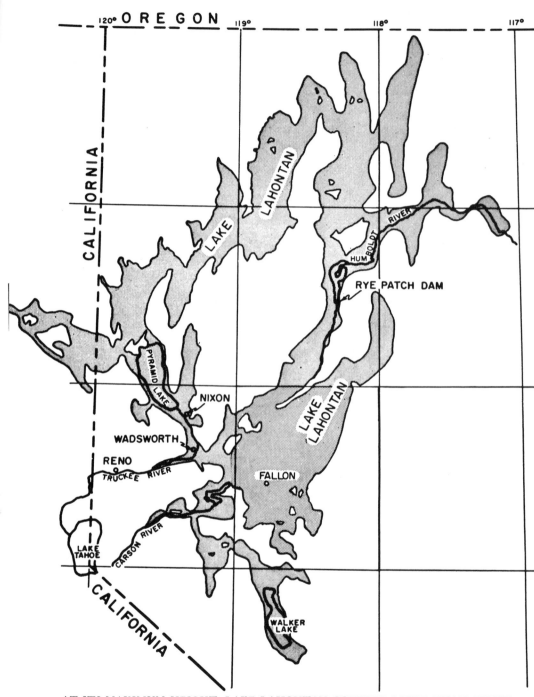

AT ITS MAXIMUM HEIGHT, LAKE LAHONTAN COVERED MORE THAN EIGHT
THOUSAND SQUARE MILES
Modified from the *Nevada Bureau of Mines Report No. 9*, by Morrison and Frye.

Americans were wandering bands of Asians who—by land, water, or ice—crossed from East Cape, Siberia, over the Bering Strait to Alaskan shores. Over thousands of years they inhabited not only the American continents but most of the adjacent islands. They prospered in the new world, and their ability to adapt to its many environments, from the Arctic to Tierra del Fuego, attests to their native intelligence.

By the time the first Europeans arrived in the Americas some of the Asian Americans had built fabulous empires. Early Spanish explorers found a dream world of Aztec palaces, art, and culture. Modern engineers stare in disbelief at the ruins of a great three-thousand-mile Inca highway, tunnels through mountains, terraced irrigation systems, and two-hundred-foot suspension bridges across canyons. Twentieth-century scientists puzzle over the evidence of delicate brain surgery performed by native Americans at a time when European doctors believed that life developed spontaneously from dead organic matter placed under a rock. Mathematicians know that the zero was used by Central Americans a thousand years before the Arabs had it, and are amazed by their knowledge of the calendar and astronomy. Agriculturists credit the native American with providing the modern world with such staples as potatoes, corn, beans, chocolate, peanuts, quinine, and rubber. And even in one of the harshest North American desert environments, the Europeans found cities of multistoried houses, complex languages allowing expression of abstract thought, artistic basketry, efficient weapons, delicately woven textiles and nets, and gentle religious philosophies showing love of nature and family.

It is often asked whether the Northern Paiute Indians who lived at Pyramid Lake when the white man first arrived there are direct descendents of the first Asian explorers of Lake Lahontan.

Present-generation Paiute elders, when shown ancient artifacts, often say, "They were made by the people before us."

And they are probably correct. Recent cave excavations indicate that the Northern Paiutes may not have come to Pyramid Lake until about A.D. 1400.

But it is also believed that all native Americans, incorrectly named Indians by early Europeans, are descendents of the migrant Asians. And in this respect the fierce Sioux warrior, the Arctic Eskimo, the Inca engineer, and the desert dwellers of the Great Basin were one people—their ancestors were of the same race.

Recent Archaeological Studies

The story which the archaeology of northwestern Nevada is beginning to tell is a fascinating one—a mystery story filled with the enchantment of the unknown. During the 1950's and early 1960's, the Nevada State Museum explored habitation and burial caves in the mountains surrounding Winnemucca Lake (Pyramid's sister lake) ; and in 1965, under the direction of its Curator of Archaeology, Donald R. Tuohy, the museum began an extensive project to excavate caves of the Pyramid Lake basin. These studies, along with prior discoveries in the Fallon and

Courtesy Frank Johnson, "Nevada State Journal"
AN ANCIENT CIVILIZATION
Members of the Lovelock Culture lived for perhaps 3,500 years among the odd-shaped
tufa formations of Pyramid Lake.

Courtesy Frank Johnson, "Nevada State Journal"
ARCHAEOLOGIST DONALD TUOHY EXAMINES A CAVE APARTMENT

Courtesy Frank Johnson, "Nevada State Journal"
FOR THOUSANDS OF YEARS THESE CAVES PROVIDED SHELTER FOR PEOPLE LIVING ALONG THE SHORES OF THE DESERT LAKE

Lovelock areas, indicate that between 9500 B.C. and A.D. 1400 at least three different prehistoric human cultures moved into and then left northwestern Nevada. There are many missing pages in the prehistory of the first two cultures but the recent excavations at Pyramid Lake have provided interesting evidence of how the third group lived for approximately 3,500 years.

Slicing down through the deep layers of thousands of years of windblown dust, so dry that decay organisms were unable to carry out their normal life processes, Tuohy's team, made up of Paiute Indians and students from several Western universities, obtained tools, weapons, foods, clothing, and even mummified bodies from the approximately ninety caves and rock shelters which they excavated. This material, pieced together with surface evidence, has allowed scientists to theorize when and how a population of humans, named by modern archaeologists the Lovelock Culture, inhabited the Pyramid Lake basin.

The people of the Lovelock Culture may have arrived at the desert lake about four thousand years ago, taking shelter in caves, many of which had been formed from the erosion of tufa rock by the waves of a higher lake. Burials indicate that the Lovelock Culture people were relatively short in stature in comparison with the Northern Paiutes who succeeded them. For warmth they dressed in robes of pelican skins and mammal pelts, wore hats made of basketry, and fashioned moccasins of buckskin.

Of perhaps the greatest interest to archaeologists is the evidence that these people exhibited some of the

Courtesy Frank Johnson, "Nevada State Journal"
WHEN PYRAMID LAKE WAS HIGHER, THIS STONE WALL MAY HAVE BEEN A
BREAKWATER FROM WHICH LOVELOCK CULTURE PEOPLE LAUNCHED
THEIR RAFTS

Courtesy Frank Johnson, "Nevada State Journal"
BECAUSE THIS LINE OF WHITE STONES SHOULD BE RUNNING PARALLEL
TO THE SHORELINE RATHER THAN AT A RIGHT ANGLE TO IT, IT IS
BELIEVED THAT THE ROCKS WERE MOVED INTO PLACE BY EARLY MEN—
PERHAPS TO BUILD A COMMUNITY FISH TRAP

elementary traits of a modern human society. Surrounding the lake, they apparently lived in community groups of three or four families, and near the
mouth of the Truckee River there are indications
that a larger settlement may have existed. The remnants of stone piers, thought to be community fish
traps, and rock breakwaters which could have protected rafts used to raid Anaho Island bird rookeries
indicate that these early people worked together to
provide a stable food supply. The many caches of
stored foods (dried fish and seeds) which cave excavations have yielded suggest that they did develop
ways of obtaining ample food—a factor which would
allow them to remain settled in one place for several
thousand years.

There may have been specialization of labor with
skilled artisans furnishing some of the more technical
necessities for their way of life. Their great fishnets,
expertly constructed of strong and uniform cord made
of plant fibers and weighted with grooved or drilled
stones, compare favorably with modern seines. Delicately woven baskets and finely chipped spearpoints
and knife blades may show the pride of accomplish-
ment of the community's specialized craftsmen and
may also suggest a stable economy which allowed
enough leisure time for artistic expression. Pacific
Ocean mollusks (abalone, olivella, and dentalium
shells), probably obtained through trade with other
tribes, furnished materials for beads and ornaments,
and interestingly, this jewelry may provide evidence
of a political or social structure. Some bodies ex-
humed by archaeologists were found to be highly em-

Courtesy Frank Johnson, "Nevada State Journal"

PETROGLYPHS ARE FOUND ON ROCKS ABOVE THE SHORES OF THE LAKE AND, THOUGH UNDECIPHERABLE, MAY HAVE BEEN ATTEMPTS AT WRITTEN COMMUNICATION

bellished with such adornments while others lacked any label of position or wealth.

In common with other primitive and civilized humans, it is probable that religious philosophies played a part in the lives of the Lovelock Culture people. Painstakingly sculptured stone effigies, some resembling local animals, have been found in the lake basin and are thought to have religious significance. Petroglyphs, which could have been primitive attempts at written communication, are found on the faces of many rocks.

All archaeological evidence indicates that the people of the Lovelock Culture lived successfully at

A SMALL HABITATION SITE

HABITATION SITE BEING EXCAVATED BY A MUSEUM ARCHAEOLOGY CREW

Courtesy Nevada State Museum
PYRAMID LAKE BASIN ARTIFACT
Atl-atl dart

Courtesy Nevada State Museum
PYRAMID LAKE BASIN ARTIFACT
Notched point

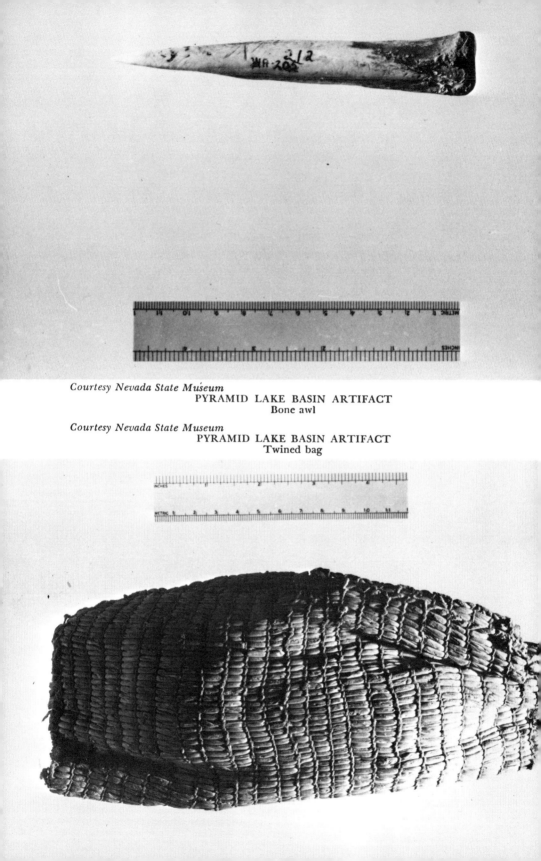

Courtesy Nevada State Museum
PYRAMID LAKE BASIN ARTIFACT
Bone awl

Courtesy Nevada State Museum
PYRAMID LAKE BASIN ARTIFACT
Twined bag

the desert lake and perhaps progressed in certain cultural and economic ways during their long stay. But did they, perhaps five hundred years ago, mysteriously disappear? Is it possible that the nomadic Northern Paiutes invaded and conquered to obtain the Great Basin's most bountiful fishery? John C. Frémont, in his narrative of his discovery of Pyramid Lake, tells of meeting "poor looking Indians" who lived in caves along the eastern side of the lake, and he indicates that they were a different tribe than the Paiutes who lived near the mouth of the river. Could these "poor looking Indians" have been the survivors of the conquered Lovelock Culture? Or, before the arrival of the Paiutes, could environmental changes, such as prolonged drouth, have forced the Lovelock Culture to leave their desert lake? Oddly enough, there is evidence that during the fifteenth century unexplained migrations occurred among other western North American tribes.

Archaeologists seek answers to these and many other prehistoric mysteries, believing that such knowledge may bring a better understanding of mankind. But the scientists face many frustrations in their important work. Amateur collectors, defying state and federal laws, dig for artifacts in Great Basin caves and, by disturbing the sediments, forever destroy vital pages in the ancient record. And while risking serious penalties and disregarding moral responsibilities, their efforts seldom produce artifacts of any value to their collections.

The people of the Lovelock Culture left to future generations a chronicle preserved in dry dust and

written in words of shell beads, broken spearpoints, basketry, pelican robes, and the remnants of fishnets. Man's curiosity, his desire to know more about the ancient past, is one of his distinctive qualities; and the prehistory story of the desert lake, if ever fully interpreted, will offer him exciting reading.

Courtesy National Park Service
THE BEAUTIFUL NEEDLES ARE NEAR THE NORTHWESTERN CORNER OF
PYRAMID LAKE

CHAPTER II

History

Discovery

On the morning of November 25, 1843, John C. Fremont and his party of twenty-four men left The Dalles on the Columbia River and traveled southward. Believing they were homeward bound, they planned a wide circular course for the purpose of exploring the Great Basin in the hope of finding the legendary Buenaventura River which was believed to flow from the Rocky Mountains to the Bay of San Francisco. Traveling down the eastern base of the Cascade Range, they passed Klamath Lake before turning east and then again south, arriving at a pass leading to the northern end of Pyramid Lake on January 10, 1844.

Captain Frémont's narrative, in part, follows:

"10th.—We continued our reconnaissance ahead, pursuing a south direction in the basin along the ridge; the camp following slowly after. On a large trail there is never any doubt of finding suitable places for encampments. We reached the end of the basin, where we found, in a hollow of the mountain which enclosed it, an abundance of good bunchgrass. Leaving a signal for the party to encamp, we continued our way up the hollow, intending to see what lay beyond the mountain. The hollow was several miles long, forming a good pass; the snow deepening to about a foot as we neared the summit. Beyond, a defile between the mountains descended rapidly about two thousand feet; and, filling up all the lower space, was a sheet of green water, some twenty miles broad. It broke upon our eyes like the ocean. The neighboring peaks rose high above us, and we ascended one of them to obtain a better view. The waves were curling in the breeze, and their dark-green color showed it to be a body of deep water. For a long time we sat enjoying the view, for we had become fatigued with mountains, and the free expanse of moving waves was very grateful. It was set like a gem in the mountains, which, from our position, seemed to enclose it almost entirely. At the western end it communicated with the line of basins we had left a few days since; and on the opposite side it swept a ridge of snowy mountains, the foot of the great Sierra. Its position at first inclined us to believe it Mary's lake, but the rugged mountains were so entirely discordant with descriptions of its low rushy shores and open country, that we concluded it some unknown body of water, which it afterwards proved to be.

"On our road down, the next day, we saw herds of mountain sheep, and encamped on a little stream at the mouth of the defile, about a mile from the margin of the water, to which we hurried down immediately. The water is so slightly salt, that, at first, we thought it fresh, and would be pleasant to drink when no other could be had. The shore was rocky—a handsome beach, which reminded us of the sea. On some large granite boulders that were scattered about the shore,

I remarked a coating of calcareous substance, in some places a few inches, and in others a foot in thickness. Near our camp, the hills, which were of primitive rock were also covered with this substance, which was in too great quantity on the mountains along the shore of the lake to have been deposited by water, and has the appearance of having been spread over the rocks in mass.

"Where we had halted appeared to be a favorite camping-place for Indians.

"13th.—We followed again a broad Indian trail along the shore of the lake to the southward. For a short space we had room enough in the bottom; but, after traveling a short distance, the water swept the foot of the precipitous mountains, the peaks of which are about 3,000 feet above the lake. The trail wound along the base of these precipices, against which the water dashed below, by a way nearly impracticable for the howitzer. During a greater part of the morning the lake was nearly hid by a snowstorm, and the waves broke on the narrow beach in a long line of foaming surf, five or six feet high. The day was unpleasantly cold, the wind driving the snow sharp against our faces; and, having advanced only about 12 miles, we encamped in a bottom formed by a ravine, covered with good grass, which was fresh and green.

"We did not get the howitzer into camp, but were obliged to leave it on the rocks until morning. We saw several flocks of sheep, but did not succeed in killing any. Ducks were riding on the waves, and several large fish were seen. The mountain sides were crusted with the calcareous cement previously mentioned. There were chenopodiaceous and other

SKETCH OF THE PYRAMID FROM FRÉMONT'S *REPORT*

shrubs along the beach; and, at the foot of the rocks, an abundance of ephedra occidentalis, whose dark-green color makes them evergreens among the shrubby growth of the lake. Towards evening the snow began to fall heavily, and the country had a wintry appearance.

"The next morning the snow was rapidly melting under a warm sun. Part of the morning was occupied in bringing up the gun; and, making only nine miles, we encamped on the shore, opposite a very remarkable rock in the lake, which had attracted our attention for many miles. It rose, according to our estimate, 600 feet above the water,* and, from the point we viewed it, presented a pretty exact outline of the great pyramid of Cheops. Like other rocks along the shore, it seemed to be incrusted with calcareous ce-

---

* According to recent measurements, the height of the pyramid above the water must have been less than 300 feet in 1844.

ment. This striking feature suggested a name for the lake, and I called it Pyramid Lake; and though it may be deemed by some a fanciful resemblance, I can undertake to say that the future traveler will find much more striking resemblance between this rock and the pyramids of Egypt, than there is between them and the object from which they take their name.

"The elevation of this lake above the sea is 4,890 feet*, being nearly 700 feet higher than the Great Salt lake, from which it lies nearly west, and distant about eight degrees of longitude. The position and elevation of this lake make it an object of geographical interest. It is the nearest lake to the western rim, as the Great Salt lake is to the eastern rim, of the Great Basin which lies between the base of the Rocky mountains and the Sierra Nevada—and the extent and character of which, its whole circumference and contents, it is so desirable to know.

"The last of the cattle which had been driven from The Dalles was killed here for food, and was still in good condition.

"15th.—A few poor looking Indians made their appearance this morning, and we succeeded in getting one into the camp. He was naked, with the exception of a tunic of hare-skins. He told us that there was a river at the end of the lake, but that he lived in the rocks near by. From the few words our people could understand, he spoke a dialect of the Snake language;

------

* This elevation could not have been correct. Geologists claim that Lahontan's elevation has not exceeded 3,950 feet in the past five thousand years. The lake's surface in 1844 has been estimated to have been about 3,860 feet above sea level. See George Hardman and Cruz Venstrom, "A One Hundred Year Record of Truckee River Runoff Estimated from Changes in Levels and Volumes of Pyramid and Winnemucca Lakes," American Geophysical Union Transactions (1941).

but we were not able to understand enough to know whether the river ran in or out, or what was its course; consequently, there still remained a chance that this might be Mary's lake.

"Groves of large cottonwood, which we could see at the mouth of the river, indicated that it was a stream of considerable size, and, at all events, we had the pleasure to know that now we were in a country where human beings could live. Accompanied by the Indian, we resumed our road, passing on the way several caves in the rock where there were baskets and seeds, but the people had disappeared. We saw also horse-tracks along the shore.

"Early in the afternoon, when we were approaching the groves at the mouth of the river, three or four Indians met us on the trail. We had an explanatory conversation in signs, and then we moved on together towards the village, which the chief said was encamped on the bottom.

"Reaching the groves, we found the inlet of a large fresh-water stream, and all at once were satisfied that it was neither Mary's river nor the waters of the Sacramento, but that we had discovered a large interior lake, which the Indians informed us had no outlet. It is about 35 miles long, and, by the mark of the water-line along the shore, the spring level is about 12 feet above its present waters. The chief commenced speaking in a loud voice as we approached; and parties of Indians, armed with bows and arrows, issued from the thickets. We selected a strong place for our encampment—a grassy bottom, nearly enclosed by the river, and furnished with abundant firewood. The village, a collection of straw huts, was a few hun-

dred yards higher up. An Indian brought in a large
fish to trade, which we had the inexpressible satisfac-
tion to find was a salmon-trout; we gathered round
him eagerly. The Indians were amused with our de-
light and immediately brought in numbers, so that the
camp was soon stocked. Their flavor was excellent—
superior, in fact, to that of any fish I have ever known.
They were of extraordinary size—about as large as the
Columbia River salmon—generally from two to four
feet in length. From the information of Mr. Walker,
who passed among some lakes lying more to the east-
ward, this fish is common to the streams of the inland
lakes. He subsequently informed me that he had obtained them weighing six pounds when cleaned and
the head taken off, which corresponds very well with
the size of those obtained at this place. They doubt-
less formed the subsistence of these people, who hold
the fishery in exclusive possession.

"I remarked that one of them gave a fish to the
Indian we had first seen, which he carried off to his
family. To them it was probably a feast; being of the
Digger tribe and having no share in the fishery, living
generally on seeds and roots. Although this was a time
of the year when the fish have not yet become fat, they
were excellent, and we could only imagine what they
are at the proper season. These Indians . . . appeared
to live an easy and happy life. They crowded into the
camp more than was consistent with our safety, re-
taining always their arms; and, as they made some
unsatisfactory demonstrations, they were given to
understand that they would not be permitted to come
armed into the camp; and strong guards were kept
with the horses. Strict vigilance was maintained

THE TUFA DEPOSITS TAKE MANY FORMS
Pictured here is "The Stone Mother and Her Basket"

among the people, and one-third at a time were kept on guard during the night. . . .

"In the mean time, such a salmon-trout feast as is seldom seen was going on in our camp; and every variety of manner in which fish could be prepared—boiled, fried, and roasted in the ashes—was put into requisition; and every few minutes an Indian would be seen running off to spear a fresh one. Whether these Indians had seen whites before, we could not be certain; but they were evidently in communication with others who had, as one of them had some brass buttons, and we noticed several other articles of civilized manufacture. We could obtain from them but little information respecting the country. They made on the ground a drawing of the river, which they represented as issuing from another lake in the mountains three or four days distant, in a direction a little west of south; beyond which, they drew a mountain; and further still, two rivers; on one of which they told us that people like ourselves traveled."

There is interesting information in these few pages of Frémont's report. His observations of mountain sheep where they no longer exist, his belief that two different tribes inhabited the basin, his descriptions of the Indians and the physical features of the area are of interest to the historian, the archaeologist, the naturalist, and to other students of the desert lake.

The Northern Paiute Indians
From 1844 through the 1860's, the history of Pyramid Lake is largely an account of its native

people and their attempt to maintain their way of life in contention with the white invasion of northwestern Nevada. The Pyramid Lake band of Northern Paiute were known as the Kuyuidokado, which in their unwritten language meant *Cui-ui,* "fish eaters." The *Cui-ui* (now pronounced "Quee-wee"), is a member of the sucker fish family, and for centuries, along with the native cutthroat trout, it furnished food for the Pyramid Lake Indians.

Many nineteenth-century writings reveal the white man's respect for the Paiutes of western Nevada, northeastern California, and southern Oregon. Indian Agent Major Frederick Dodge, in 1859, estimated that they numbered from 6,000 to 7,000 people and said that they "resemble in appearance, manner, and customs, the Delawares of our Missouri frontier." United States Senate Documents of 1859-60, the Thirty-sixth Congress, record Major Dodge's belief that they "are undoubtedly the most interesting and docile Indians on the continent."

Other early observers described these desert people as tall, with long, thin faces; and they praised their intelligence, morality, trustworthiness, industry, and horsemanship.

In 1865 Indian Agent Franklin Campbell wrote the Commissioner of Indian Affairs in Washington, D.C., "I have been the local Ind. Agt. on this reserve since April 1st 1862 up to the present time, fifteen months excepted. This constant life among the Pi-Utes has enabled me to become acquainted with them both personally and generally throughout the tribe, and also to form opinions based on experiences as to their true character, better perhaps than any other man in the State.

"On the whole they are as honest, and truthfull. . . . They are good reasoners and thinkers and are generally kind and humane. . . . As yet they have resisted the harmful influences of intoxicating drink and have preserved with great tenacity the native virtue of their women."

The report of the Commissioner of Indian Affairs for 1871 contains a statement that the Paiute Indians were, "superior in intelligence and culture," and includes, "Their manifest regard for their females is remarkable indeed. . . . I have been told repeatedly that of the more than 5,000 Paiute Indians, there is not a mixed blood among them and I have seen nothing to contradict it."

In 1876, Dan De Quille (William Wright) wrote in *The Big Bonanza,* "Very few Paiutes will touch whiskey or liquor of any kind. The women are remarkable for their chastity, and are in this respect models . . . for those of all nations and colors."

Although during the 1850's there were many Indian raids on California-bound emigrants crossing Nevada, records show that as late as the spring of 1860 the Paiutes, with the exception of several northern renegade bands, remained at peace with the white man. Honey Lake Valley, located to the northwest of Pyramid Lake, became an area of white settlement relatively close to the lake, and a statement made by one of the valley's early settlers, Captain Weatherlow, included in a report from Colonel Frederick W. Lander

SOME OF THE ELDERLY PAIUTES STILL USE THE OLD METHODS OF GATHER-
ING AND PREPARING THE NUTS OF THE PINON PINE

to the United States Commissioner of Indian Affairs,
reveals Indian-white relationships during that decade.
In Captain Weatherlow's account, the name "Winnemucca" obviously refers to Young Winnemucca,
whose Indian name was Numaga. Numaga was the
leader of the Pyramid Lake Paiutes but was known
to the whites as the Paiute war chief. The other
Winnemucca (Poito), known to the whites as the
"Medicine Man," is called Old Winnemucca throughout Colonel Lander's report.

"Statement of Capt. Weatherlow.
"In the month of June 1856 I settled in Honey

Lake Valley. There were but two or three houses there at that time. The Pah-ute tribe of Indians occupied the valley in common with the whites, and were upon the most friendly terms with them, visiting the houses of the whites and trading furs and game for such articles of clothing &c as they desired. They were unlike other tribes which I had met in the country in as much as they were never known to beg for food or clothing nor did they at every opportunity pilfer and carry off articles from the settlement. They were under the command and control of Winnemucca the present war Chief and faithfully obeyed his orders. There was a small band however which lived in or near Smoke Creek Canon [Canyon] and were under the control of a Chief known as Smoke Creek Sam. [T]hese had in a measure drawn away from Winnemucca's band, and although still on friendly terms with Winnemucca's people they were in a degree independent of his control. In the year 1855 the settlers of the valley made a treaty with the Chief Winnemucca, the terms of which were that if any Indian committed any depredation or stole any thing from the whites, the settler should go to the chief and make complaint to him and not take their [sic] revenge indiscriminately upon the Indians, and the whites on their part agreed that if a white man should steal horses or cattle from the Indians or molest their squaws that the chief should come and make his complaint and the settler would redress his wrongs and punish the offender. The settlers also passed a resolution that no white man should molest or live with a squaw in the valley under penalty of being summarily dealt with and driven from the Settlement. The treaty was faithfully observed on both sides, and never in a single instance was there a misunderstanding between the whites and Indians.

"From the first settlement of the valley the Pitt River Indians which inhabit the Country north of Honey Lake had made frequent incursions upon the settlements—driven off stock and committed other outrages. In the year 1857, I raised a company of 60 men and went out against the Pitt River tribe on several occasions when they had made descent upon the valley—Winnemucca volunteered to go with his warriors and aid us in fighting the Pitt River Indians —his offer wa[s] accepted and he and his warriors placed themselves under my command and rendered most efficient service; he obeyed orders strictly and fought as bravely as any white man; he was also of great service in giving me information in regard to the hostile tribe; the[i]r places of retreat, &c. On one occasion we succeeded in surprising some three hundred of the Pitt River Indians as they were in the act of massacring a small train of Mormon Emigrants; we mad[e] a descent upon the Indians, killed some 25 of them and put the rest to flight, recovered the stock they had stolen and escorted the emigrant families to the settlement.

"By these frequent attacks and by the efficient aids of Winnemucca and his warriors we finally scattered the Pitt River tribe and they have never since made an incursion upon the valley.

"The friendly relations between the Settlers and the Pah-ute were greatly strengthened from the fact that Winnemucca had aided us in this war with the Pitt River tribe. In the spring of 1858 I started with four men on a prospecting trip to the Black Rock County [Country]. Two days after we left Honey Lake Peter Lasser* an old mountaineer and settler left the valley in company with two men to overtake and join us; we reached our place of destination two days in advance of them and were encamped on a hill about 7 miles from mud [Quinn River]** Lake. Lassers party followed our trail and arrived within a mile of our camp when darkness overtook them and they halted for the night at the mouth of a small canon [cañon] near the foot of the mountain. The next day they sent out one of their party to search for our camp but unfortunately he missed our trail and returned to Lasser's camp saying that he could not find us. They passed another night in the canon [sic] and at daybreak they were attacked by a party of Indians and Pete Lasser with one other man was killed. The third man suceeded [sic] in mounting his horse without saddle or bridle and thinking our party had also been massacred [sic] he made his way directly to Honey Lake. I remained out with my party until our provisions grew short and supposing that Lasser's party had taken a different rout[e] we started to return knowing nothing of the murder until the second day of our travel homeward when we met a party of settlers who informed us of the massacre and that they had started out to ascertain the fate of my

---

* The misspelling of Peter Lassen's name may have been an error in transcription when Captain Weatherlow's account was included in Colonel Lander's handwritten report.

** Several bodies of water in this general region were called "Mud" lakes in the early days. It is believed that the "Mud Lake" to which Captain Weatherlow referred was probably the sink of the Quinn River.

IN ITS MOOD OF CALM, THE DESERT LAKE IS FRIENDLY

party which they feared had also been killed. The murder of Pete Lasser and his companions [sic] caused great excitement in the Settlement and much feeling against the Indians. Several of the settlers attributed the murder to the Pah-utes but from my own knowledge of the friendly relations between the Chief Winnemucca and Peter Lasser; and the high estimation in which Lasser was held by the Indians; and from the fact that there was no apparent change in the conduct of the Pah-ute who contrived to visit our houses and exchange civilities and friendships; I did not believe the Pah-utes had committed the murder nor that they were at all cognizant of the fact. I attributed it entirely to the Pitt River tribe which the whites had fought and defeated and who frequented the Black Rock Country in small bands.

"Up to the time Major Dodge the Indian Agent to the Pah-ute tribe had never visited the Valley to my knowledge; but shortly after the killing of Lasser's party he came to Honey Lake remained about one day and returned to Carson City without having had an interview with Winnemucca or made any earnest inquiry into the cause or the perpetration of the murder. The suspicion which had rested upon the minds of some the settlers that the Pah-utes had murdered Lasser gradually died away, and the same friendly relations existed as before. The treaty was respected on both sides; the Indians were kindly treated and no white man attempted to molest their squaws or wrong them in any way.

"This friendly state of affairs continued until the discovery of rich silver beds in the Washoe Country

A STORM MOVES OVER THE DESERT LAKE

It is hoped that future development of the basin will be carefully planned to preserve the primitive atmosphere which makes the desert lake so unusual. Without that distinctive quality it would lose its charm and, consequently, its economic value.

brought a host of miners and prospectors and adven-
turers of every kind to Carson and Virginia City, who
were brought in contact more or less with the Pah-
ute tribe, and who, knowing nothing of the treaty
which the Honey Lake people had made with Winnemucca or caring nothing to observe it, frequently
treated the Indians with injustice and cruelty. The
Pah-ute bitterly complained to us of their wrongs and
evidently expected that the terms of our treaty should
extend to the whites who were flocking into the
Southern portion of the Territory.

"Of course the people of Honey Lake could offer
them no redress nor interpose in their behalf.

"Winnemucca and his people notwithstanding the
difficulty they were frequently having with the people
of Virginia City, and the prospecting parties through
the mountains, still remained in apparent friendship
toward the people of Honey Lake, but the same earnest feeling of confidence in the justice of the whites
did not exist—the red man according to his nature and
teaching held any and every white man in a measure
responsible for the wrongs he had received at the
hands of any unprincipled white man. Still no threats
had been made toward the settlers nor had any overt
act of hostility been done towards us by the Pah-utes
until the month of January 1860 when Dexter E.
Deming a young man who resided on Willow Creek
about 10 miles from Honey Lake was attacked by a
party of Indians when alone in his cabin and murdered; his horses stolen and his cabin rifled.

"The news of this outrage greatly excited the
people of Honey Lake—they demanded that I should

take my company which was still under organization
and march out against the Pah-utes as they were con-
fident the Pah-utes had committed the murder. I told
them that the Pah-utes had always been friendly and
as there existed a treaty between Winnemucca and
ourselves which had never been broken, it was better
to go and see the Chief and learn the truth of the
matter. I believe it might have been the Pitt River
tribe who frequently made hunting excursions so far
south as Willson Creek. A meeting of citizens was
then held and it was agreed that I should send the
Lieutenant of my company with 15 men to trace the
murderers and ascertain if it was the Pah-utes or Pitt
River Indians. The party were out four days; tracked
the Indians through the snow; recovered the horses
and came back reporting that it was the Pah-utes
known as the Smoke Creek band which had drawn
away from Winnemucca's control and recognized
Smoke Creek Sam as their leader.

"Another meeting was then held and they again demanded that I should take my company and march
out against the Pah-utes. I told them that at that time
there were three thousand head of stock at Pyramid
Lake protected by only a few herders. There were
settlers located in small valleys remote from each other
and distant from the settlements at Honey Lake—and
that small parties of prospectors were scattered
through the mountains in every direction, all of whom
would be hopelessly exposed and murdered if I made
an attack upon the Indians at that time. It was then
agreed that I should go and have an interview with
Winnemucca, inform him of the murder and demand

redress. I went in company with Mr. Thomas J. Harvey as a commissioner from the Gov- of the Territory, Isaac Roop Esqr on behalf of the people of the valley. On the third day of our travel we were met by a band of about thirty Pah-ute Indians well armed and mounted who surrounded us and took us prisoners thus preventing our proceeding to the main camp. They kept close watch over us during the night, and in the morning allowed us to depart but refused to give any information as to the whereabouts of their Chief. These Indians were also of the Smoke Creek band and their endeavor was evidently to prevent our having an interview with Winnemucca. They told us in plain terms that we should not see him but must go back to Honey Lake if we valued our lives. We started in the direction of Honey Lake and travelled a few miles when we took advantage of a dense fog which hid our movements from the view of the Indians and made our way across the country to the Truckee River which we followed down to Pyramid Lake. We found camps of Indians scattered along at intervals but they refused to give us any information as to the whereabouts of Winnemucca. We proceeded down the Lake to another Indian encampment where we found the Chief with some forty warriors. Winnemucca welcomed us and spread a blanket for us to sit down in his own tent.

"We told him our errand and that we demanded of him the delivery of the murderer or murderers of D. E. Deming in accordance with the terms of the treaty entered into between his people and the whites. At the same time we invited Winnemucca and the other Chiefs to return with us to the valley and settle our difficulties amicably.

"Winnemucca acknowledged that in accordance with the treaty we were justified in making the demand as he neither admitted nor denied that the Pahutes had committed the murder. . . ."

Captain Weatherlow's statement indicates the gradual deterioration of trust between white and Indian during the 1850's—a process which reached its climax at Pyramid Lake in the spring of 1860 and resulted in one of the most spectacular but tragic events in Nevada's history.

The Battles of Pyramid Lake

Preserved in National Archive microfilms, 1860 California newspaper files, Nevada history books, and other documents can be found many accounts, often conflicting, of the first battle of Pyramid Lake in which more white men died than in any prior white-Indian engagement in the Far West.

In May of 1860, unknown to the white people of the region, Paiute Indians from throughout much of their range had gathered at Pyramid Lake to consider the white invasion which threatened to destroy their way of life. In addition to the many Paiute bands, a number of Bannock and Shoshone Indians attended the council.

Except for Numaga (Young Winnemucca), all of the band leaders were in favor of war. Numaga, described by a Sacramento newspaper reporter who interviewed him as "not just a superior Indian; he is a superior man of any race," was highly respected by his people, and his arguments as to the hopelessness of conflict might have swayed the council—if the Williams' station massacre had not occurred.

There are conflicting versions as to why an Indian war party killed four white men and burned Williams' station, a whiskey shop on the emigrant road along the bank of the Carson River. Some accounts claim that the raid was made without cause by a renegade band from the north, but the story that the white men held two Indian women captive is generally considered the most reasonable explanation.

When news of the killings reached the Indian council at Pyramid Lake, Numaga is reported to have said, "There is no longer any use for counsel; we must prepare for war, for the soldiers will now come here to fight us."

In the white settlements, the massacre quickly resulted in the organization of a volunteer army consisting of detachments from Genoa, Carson City, Silver City, and Virginia City; and on May 9, 1860, 105 poorly armed men began the march toward Williams' station. Although Major Ormsby has been reported the leader of the volunteer army, there was no central command, and a lack of discipline, as well as a failure to realize the need of it, probably was characteristic of most of the men.

Arriving at Williams' station the next day, the volunteers found and buried the bodies of three men and voted to continue on to Pyramid Lake.

On the night of May 11 the party camped at the present site of Wadsworth and the next morning re-

Thompson and West, History of Nevada
NUMAGA, THE GREAT INDIAN LEADER DURING THE
BATTLES OF PRYAMID LAKE
Called "Young Winnemucca" by the whites, historians have often con-
fused him with Poito (Old Winnemucca), who was known as the
"Medicine Man" of the Paiutes.

sumed their march north, following an Indian trail
along the plateau on the east side of the Truckee
River. At a point approximately ten miles from the
lake, where a steep mountain slope cuts through the
plateau down to the river, the trail narrows; and here
several men were stationed to hold off a pursuing
force if an unexpected retreat should become necessary.

South of where the highway now passes through
Nixon, the river gorge widens into meadows, and the
trail drops down from the higher tableland to the
level of the river. The volunteers had proceeded a
short distance beyond the present location of Nixon
when they sighted a line of horse-mounted Indians,
just out of gunshot range, on an elevated stretch of
land to the army's right front. The enemy appeared
to be of about the same number as the whites, increasing the confidence of the volunteers.

An order was given to dismount and tighten saddle
girths, and while this was in progress, a man with a
globe-sighted rifle fired at the Indians, apparently
without effect.

When again mounted, a detachment of about thirty
men charged toward the enemy while the remainder
of the whites followed at a slower pace. Reaching the
higher ground, the leaders were surprised to find that
the Indians had mysteriously disappeared in a terrain
which seemed to offer little opportunity for concealment. And then, again just beyond rifle range, another line of mounted warriors appeared, forming a
flanking semicircle which extended dangerously far

ON THE MORNING OF MAY 12, 1860, THE VOLUNTEER ARMY LEFT THE BIG
BEND OF THE TRUCKEE RIVER (NOW THE SITE OF WADSWORTH) AND
STARTED THEIR MARCH TO PYRAMID LAKE

THEY FOLLOWED THE OLD INDIAN TRAIL ON THE EAST SIDE
OF THE RIVER
The trail still can be seen today

THE TRAIL RAN ALONG THE PLATEAU ABOVE THE RIVER

AT A PLACE ABOUT TEN MILES FROM THE LAKE, THE TRAIL NARROWED
Here several men were stationed to hold off pursuers if an unexpected retreat should
become necessary.

to the south. As the whites paused, wondering if they had charged into a trap, the attack began.

From behind sagebrush on both sides of the forward detachment, Indians materialized and began pouring a hail of bullets and arrows into the whites. Probably, during the next few minutes, the battle was lost. The realization that they had entered a clever trap, the un-expected aggressiveness and numbers of the enemy quickly changed confidence to fear. Wounded by arrows and frightened by the war cries and gunfire, horses of the forward detachment were rearing and bucking, causing men to drop their rifles and pistols. Riders able to control their animals were wheeling them about; and within minutes the entire white army was in retreat.

The volunteers first turned toward the west, seek-shelter in the groves of cottonwood trees which lined the riverbank. But the Indian attack had been care-fully planned, and two bands of mounted warriors emerged from the trees and raced toward the whites. It was at this moment, observers claimed, that Numa-ga made his last attempt to prevent tragedy. Spurring his horse between the charging Indians and the whites, he attempted to obtain a parley; but in the confusion the Indians swept past him.

A short distance south of where the present high-way passes through Nixon, the Truckee River flowed within approximately fifty yards of an elevated stretch of land, and this was the mouth of the trap where warriors awaited. To bypass the gauntlet of bullets and arrows, one party of whites attempted to ford the river but the preceding winter had been

THE VOLUNTEERS SIGHTED A LINE OF HORSE-MOUNTED INDIANS ON
ELEVATED LAND TO THEIR RIGHT FRONT

A DETACHMENT OF THIRTY MEN CHARGED UP THIS HILLSIDE AND, ON
REACHING THE TOP, FOUND THAT THE ENEMY HAD DISAPPEARED

severe, and the Truckee was so high and swift from the melting snows of its Sierra Nevada watershed that the horses were unable to swim against the current and were swept back to the bank they had left.

Beyond the mouth of the trap, about one fourth of a mile before the trail climbed out of the meadows, surviving volunteers made a last desperate attempt at a stand. Realizing that the steep, narrow exit from the bottomland would slow the retreat, Major Ormsby sent several men ahead to take positions from which they could hold off the enemy until the main body of volunteers reached the plateau. Crawling Indians concealed by the undergrowth soon forced the whites to continue their retreat, and as the lead horses struggled up the steep path to the higher land, mounted warriors closed with the rear of the column.

The whites who reached the plateau began a race with death down the trail. Men with the fastest horses led the way, and those whose animals were unable to keep the pace gradually slipped back into the midst of the enemy. On reaching the narrow pass, where on the way out men had been stationed to secure a retreat, the lack of discipline allowed the guards to desert their posts and join the fleeing leaders.

Deep draws through the plateau, formed by the runoff of rainwater from the slopes of the mountain, were an additional hazard. Here again the lead horses were slowed by the steep banks, allowing the Indians to overtake the column.

Approximately nine miles from where the battle began, the trail passed down from the plateau to the river and crossed the bottomland for about one half mile before climbing again to the higher area. Major Ormsby, shot in the mouth and both arms, and riding a wounded mule, was climbing the trail to the plateau when he was overtaken and killed. Darkness came as survivors reached the site of Wadsworth, allowing them to scatter and escape. The exact number of white casualties was never definitely determined. Several years after the battle, Indians claimed they had counted forty-six dead volunteers. It is probable that many wounded men died somewhere between Pyramid Lake and Virginia City, for a summary of estimates indicates that at least seventy men remained unaccounted for.

When news of the disaster reached Virginia City the next day and was carried from there to California, it not only created panic in the territory but caused fear throughout the West for a general Indian uprising. At Virginia City, women and children were barricaded in an unfinished stone building and many residents quickly lost interest in their search for wealth and started over the mountains for California. At Silver City, in a stone fort overlooking Devil's Gate, a wooden cannon with iron hoops was constructed and filled with scrap iron. It was fortunate that the expected Indian attack did not occur; for when, at a later date, the cannon was fired with a slow fuse, it exploded and showered shrapnel in all directions.

Communities across the Sierra Nevadas quickly organized to assist their Nevada neighbors. Companies of well-armed volunteers were hurriedly formed in Downieville, Nevada City, San Juan, Sacramento, and Placerville. At Downieville, within thirty-six hours of receiving news of the battle, 165 men were on their way to Virginia City, which they reached five days later after marching on foot over the mountains. Four companies of regular United States Army troops, numbering 207 men, were ordered to proceed from San Francisco and Benicia to meet and join forces with the volunteers at Williams' Station on the Carson River.

Commanded by an experienced Indian fighter, Colonel John Hays, the 547 volunteers reached the rendezvous on May 28 after a march characterized by cold thunderstorms and the fatal ambush of their scout. On the next day a skirmish with a large party of mounted Indians* resulted in three wounded volunteers. The army regulars arrived that afternoon, and a march to the Big Bend of the Truckee River was made on May 31. By nighfall of June 1, a camp was established about eight miles downstream, and here a slight earthworks was constructed which was later named Fort Storey, in honor of Captain Storey who was killed in the ensuing battle.

The next morning a detachment of eighty mounted men was detailed to proceed toward Pyramid Lake under orders to fall back to the main camp if attacked. Passing the bodies of men killed in the first battle, the detachment reached the point where the trail dropped down from the plateau to the wide meadows. Here a portion of the command remained on the high ground while a scouting party went ahead.

The scouts had traveled only a short distance across the meadows when they received a signal from the plateau that Indians, moving up the valley, had been

---

*Colonel Hays commentated that these Paiute riders were among the finest horsemen he had ever seen.

sighted. Approximately three hundred horse-mounted warriors were advancing in the form of a wedge and were followed by Indians on foot. An orderly retreat of the whites soon brought them within sight of the main body of troops advancing to meet them.

The battle was fought along the plateau and the steep side of the mountain. Troops and volunteers formed a mile-long line and gradually fought their way northward. To those who witnessed the battle and to the historians who later recorded it, the Indians' defense was amazing. Using methods of concealment learned through centuries of stalking game in the barren Great Basin, they held off the white army long enough for the main body of Indian women, children, and men to escape to northern regions. Several accounts claim that Numaga directed the warriors by signaling with a white flag (probably a pelican wing) from a mountain peak overlooking the battlefield.

Because the Indians carried their dead and wounded with them as they retreated, the number of their casualties was never definitely determined. Accounts indicate at least three whites were killed and five wounded.

On the fourth of June a detachment of the white army moved north to Pyramid Lake but found the Paiute village deserted. The Indian trail led northward along the west side of Winnemucca Lake, and while following it, a scout was killed in one of the canyons of the mountains which separate Pyramid and Winnemucca lakes.

No further contact with the Indians was made, and on June 7 the volunteers were disbanded. A detachment of regular army troops remained at Pyramid until the middle of July, constructing earthworks which received the name of Fort Haven.

During the remainder of 1860 Fort Churchill on the Carson River was constructed, and a peace treaty with the Paiutes was negotiated by Colonel Frederick W. Lander. Colonel Lander, superintendent of the emigrant road, met with Numaga at a hot springs on the emigrant road; and portions of his report, recorded on National Archive microfilm, provide interesting observations of the Paiute Indians.

From Colonel Lander's Report

". . . They arrived there early in the day designated, bringing with them the Chief and four of his principal warriors.

"Winnemucka [Numaga] said he would look hard at me and when the sun was low would be ready to talk. The council, which was held at sunset, lasted over an hour and was quite an interesting one.

"I told the Chief that I came to hear him say all he had to tell the great Father of the whites. I would listen with attention, but that I was only a listener. I could make him no promises. When the great Father heard from his children, the Pah-utes, he would then know what to do. Perhaps he might be very angry because his people had been killed. He might send many warriors to fight the Indians and kill them, the Chief must talk plain, he must hide nothing. I should listen to him with open ears.

"His reply was characteristic of the better class Indians of the plains. He said that when he asked me to wait until night before he would talk it was not because he liked the darkness. His heart was very open, it was like the sunshine, but some clouds had been before him, many of his young men had been killed, and he saw in my train men who had killed them, his breath was hot, it might have burnt my ears had he spoken too soon, now he had sat upon my blanket, had eaten of my meat and at last had smoked the pipe, and was quiet so that he could talk calmly.

"He then waited for me to reply. I remarked that I brought with me to see him John Deming, the brother of the white man whom the Pah-Utes killed last winter, when no war existed, whose house they had burned, whose horses and arms they had stolen, who was now a very poor man with nothing left but his powder, his bullets and his gun with which he wished to fight the Pah-Utes forever.

"This man, whose heart was hardened against them, had much more cause to complain than the Indians had: none of his family had ever killed a Pah-Ute and if any of my men had killed them it was because the Pah-Utes had fired at our party and shot down a comrade when I was seeking a peaceful interview.

"I told him that I was very glad my young men had killed some Pah-Utes and to day I came to see him with warriors, not with squaws. If he wished to talk to woman, and if it made his heart bad to see my men, I would go home and send a woman to him.

"He then wished to see Deming and looked at him very steadfastly for some moments but at the time said nothing. He then addressed the Indians who were present very vehemently in his own language.

"The interpreter told me that in his harangue he denounced 'Smoke Creek Sam' of the Pah-Utes, and the Chief of a wandering band of Oregon Snakes and border Pah-Utes called 'Mackaw,' saying that with these Indians lay the blame of Deming[']s death. . . . The Chief then turned to me and said, 'Is Winnemucka a woman that he should *go to council with woman*? No! he is a man!' (striking his breast), 'and the whites know it, They have never heard him cry, —no not once. Ten, twelve snows have fallen since they came to see Winnemucka. They were few and they were very poor. They asked the Pah-Utes for land. They said they would make flour for the Indians. They would give them blankets and powder and lead, and that the pappooses [*sic*] and squaws should be fed. Until last year no trouble had occur[r]ed, but the whites had been very mean and had not kept their promises. They had accused him of killing Pete Lassen, one of the best men he ever knew, with whom he had slept in the same blanket, who was like an Indian and had lived among them before the other white people came. During all this time the whites had received more than they had given. It was not their country but his. The whites had taken the Indians' ponies and their buck-skins and often failed in their obligations to pay. White men had been to him like coyotes, always ready to eat and to bark; they made a heap of talk and much of their talk was not good.' He dwelt bitterly and frequently upon the promises made to him and broken, and said he was glad at last to see a white man who came without promises.

"He then spoke again very earnestly to the Indians with him.

"By aid of the interpreter I was informed that he had again reverted to the fact of the first massacre having been committed by wandering bands beyond his control. He then asked me if the great Father could manage all the whites. I told him that he usually could, but that there were bad whites as well as bad Indians. He said that the poor Indians . . . the Diggers of California, had been put by the great Father on reserved lands where, after their country was taken from them, they were to have been fed by the whites; that they had got very hungry and killed some cattle for food where-upon the whites had murdered them all, men, women and children. What had I to say to this? Was it not better for him to fight while the whites were few in his country and to die with his arms in his hands, and his young men to die with him? To be sure it was. He was sorry for the women and children who would starve in the mountains, but if they were all to die, why not perish before they were shut up by the whites and their arms taken from them. It was very difficult for me to reply to this, for the last year's massacres of reserve Indians in northern California are a dead weight on explanations made to these fierce tribes of the plains. The latter are apprised by runners of all such occurrences and I believe that the knowledge of these murders has had much to do with the present war. I told the Chief that his tribe was more like the whites than the Daggers [sic]. That much of the Pah-Ute territory, especially the mountain-sheep and antelope ranges, the whites would never covet, that their lakes were full of fish which the whites did not want. That they, the Pah-Utes were good riders and herders and, if once furnished with cattle and taught how to farm, would take care of themselves.

"I described to him the happiness of the Cherokees, Winnebagoes, Delawares and other Indians whom the whites had taught to farm.

"He said he had heard all this before, but even if he was willing to go on a reserve with his people, have cattle and ploughs, and a mill to make flour, he had waited too long and the good white man who was to be sent by the great Father to teach him never came and the reserve was never provided. He then sat quiet for a space of time silent and with his head bent down apparently in deep thought. . . . He said the Pah-Utes had been shot and their women ravished without his fighting, that the son of one of his Chiefs had been killed at Virginia City, and that still he did not really wish to fight. . . .

"The terms of the armistice, which was the result of this conversation, provided that the Pah-Utes abstain from all acts of hostility against the whites for one year, or until the grass is dry next summer. This only under the express condition, that the whites in like manner abstain from aggression on them. In the meantime I promised to relate his story to the great Father at Washington and if possible get a treaty confirmed within the time mentioned. Winnemucka immediately sent runners to Oregon for the Medicine man, or old Chief Winnemucka [Poito], who, it is reported, has always been averse to the war. He said

the old man would arrive in two weeks and, with him-
self, would await Major Dodge[']s arrival at the lower
Big Meadows on the Humboldt. The war Chief
promised me in the meantime immediately to visit
Fort Churchill."

History records that this meeting between Numaga
and Colonel Lander was the beginning of peace between the white man and the main body of the
Northern Paiute of Pyramid.

In September of 1860, Warren Wasson, a romantic
figure in Nevada's history, became acting Indian agent
and, trusted by the Indians, was influential in main-
taining peace. Most historians mention the story of
the Paiute gathering in December of 1860 at which
Wasson gave clothing to the men and sewing materials
to the women. After his presents were exhausted, an
old man arrived at the meeting, and the Indians
watched to see what Wasson would do. All were im-
pressed when he stripped off his own shirt and
drawers and gave them to the old Paiute.

In May of 1862, Wasson arranged for Territorial
Governor Nye to meet with the Indians. Governor
Nye, escorted by a force of one hundred cavalry, arrived at the site of Wadsworth on the twenty-third
of May and was met there by Wasson, Old Winnemucca, and four hundred Paiute warriors. According
to Nevada historians, the meeting was colorful, with
the Indians performing war dances and undergoing
torture to impress the whites with their indifference
to pain. Numaga arrived on the night of the twenty-

CALIFORNIA AND NEVADA INDIANS MADE BEAUTIFUL BASKETS

fifth, and with him Governor Nye discussed the various problems of the Indians.

As a sign of peace and friendship, Numaga gave Wasson a magnificent bow with arrows and quiver, his war cap made of whole otter skin and trimmed with eagle plumes, and his combination tomahawk and peace pipe. The last article is presently on display at the Nevada State Museum.

Indian-white warfare continued during the 1860's throughout much of northern Nevada; but in general, the Kuyuidokado, though faced with many frustrations, attempted to retain their rights and their desert lake by use of the white man's courts and legislative bodies instead of by arrows and bullets.

The Pyramid Lake Reservation

Records show that on November 25, 1859, Frederick Dodge, Western Utah Territory Agent for the United States Office of Indian Affairs, wrote a letter to the Commissioner of Indian Affairs, Mr. A. B. Greenwood, asking that the northern portion of the Truckee River Valley, including Pyramid Lake, be reserved for Indians. On November 29, 1859, Mr. Greenwood then requested by a letter to Samuel A. Smith, Commissioner of the United States General Land Office, that Mr. Smith direct the Surveyor-General of Utah Territory to respect this reservation, "upon the plats of survey when the public surveys shall have been extended over that part of the territory, and in the meantime the proper local land officers may be instructed to respect the reservation

CAPTAIN DAVE NUMANANA SUCCEEDED WINNEMUCCA IN 1879
AS THE PRINCIPAL LEADER OF THE PYRAMID LAKE INDIANS
Captain Dave claimed that he was born in 1829 and that he remembered
Frémont. He died on his Pyramid ranch in 1919.

upon the books of their offices when such offices shall have been established."

However, the Executive Order, which follows, was not made until March 23, 1874.

The President

March 23, 1874

EXECUTIVE MANSION

It is hereby ordered that the tract of country known and occupied as the Pyramid Lake Indian Reservation in Nevada, as surveyed by Eugene Moore, in January, 1865, and indicated by red lines, according to the courses and distances given in tabular form on accompanying diagrams, be withdrawn from sale or other disposition, and set apart for the Pah-Ute and other Indians residing thereon.

U. S. GRANT

Although the reservation, including the lake, totaled 475,152 acres, only a small percentage of the area was irrigable; and during the more than fourteen years between 1859 and President Grant's 1874 executive order, a number of white settlers located much of the land suitable for farming and ranching. Records show that in 1861 Territorial Governor Nye wrote the Secretary of the Interior that he had found ranches and white settlers on the reservation and said, "I have instructed the agent to warn them off, which he has done." Sixty-three years later, the whites still occupied these lands.

In 1924 the United States Congress passed legislation which allowed the white families to acquire legal title to the lands they held by purchase at an established price. However, five of the white ranchers did not complete their payments, and, in 1942, a U.S.

Courtesy Mrs. R. H. Cowles Collection
A YOUNG PAIUTE MOTHER AND HER BABY

Circuit Court of Appeals awarded their holdings to the Pyramid Lake tribe.

Early Settlements

One of the first ranches in the Pyramid Lake basin was located in 1864 by Charles Symonds. According to his grandson, Verne Whittey, of Reno, Mr. Symonds came from Boston to Virginia City, where he operated freight teams hauling ore. In July of 1864, he began building a house at the lower end of the meadow of Big Canyon Creek, about thirteen miles north of Sutcliffe on the west side of the lake. The "Symonds' Place," constructed with lumber hauled from Virginia City, became a stage station on the main road from Reno to Surprise Valley and Fort Bidwell. It was called a "breakfast station" because stages leaving Reno in the evening arrived at the Symonds station the next morning; and, while the four-horse teams were being replaced with fresh animals, the stage passengers were served breakfast. Many soldiers, en route to Fort Bidwell, stopped overnight at the Symonds' Place, which eventually became the Pyramid Post Office and Pyramid station on the railroad.

Charles Symonds' daughter Elizabeth was the first white child born on the reservation. She married James Whittey, and the ranch is still owned and operated by descendants of the original settler.

Sutcliffe, also on the west side of the lake, was known in early days as "The Willows." James Sutcliffe, according to records furnished by his niece, Mrs. Maude Heller, came west from Rhode Island to

Courtesy Mrs. R. H. Cowles Collection
FRANK NORTHRUP, A HIGHLY RESPECTED PAIUTE
He was born at Pyramid in the early 1840's and remembered the white
migrations through Nevada. He was a ranch foreman in Suprise Valley
and a wrangler for the the big R. H. Cowles ranch near Pyramid.

AN INDIAN HOME AT WADSWORTH IN THE EARLY 1900's

California in 1857, and moved to the Virginia City area in 1862. His wife Margaret J. Sutcliffe, as a small girl traveled with her parents by ship around the Horn and settled in Dayton. In 1885, the Sutcliffes built a stage station at Pyramid, which later became a popular resort for Nevadans and tourists. In 1945, Harry and Joan Drackert leased the Sutcliffe resort and operated it until 1956 as a widely known guest ranch as well as a place to breed and raise descendants of the famous quarter horse, Peter McCue.

The third and only other existing settlement in the lake's basin is the Indian community of Nixon, and its beginning probably dates back to prehistoric times. Located at the south end of Pyramid Lake, it may

PAIUTE BABY SNUGLY LACED IN ITS CARRYING BASKET

PAIUTE INDIAN WOMAN OF THE PYRAMID LAKE RESERVATION

have been the site of the Indian village which Frémont visited in 1844. In the 1870's the reservation's
headquarters and school were built at Nixon, and it
became the central community for the Indian ranches
of the vicinity.

Mining

Prospecting, strictly within the Pyramid basin, has
never developed a productive mine. However, according to a bulletin written by F. C. Lincoln in 1923,
the Pyramid Mining District, located a few miles west
of the lake, has produced silver-bearing copper ore
which contained some gold. Although known as early
as 1860, the district did not become active until 1876
when the Monarch mine was located and a stamp mill
erected. The mining community was called Pyramid
City and, like the Symonds' Place, was a stage stop
where horses were replaced by a fresh team. The
Pyramid Mining District has been active at intervals
up until the present.

After 1900

In 1912 the Southern Pacific Company began con-
struction of a railway line from Fernley, Nevada, to
Westwood, California. Routed through the Pyramid
basin on the west side of the lake, the tracks reached
the Red River Lumber Company at Westwood early
in 1914. Constructed primarily to transport lumber,
the railway also provided passenger service, allowing
many people to enjoy the scenery of Pyramid Lake.

During World War II, the Naval Auxiliary Air
Station near Fallon, Nevada, used the lake for torpedo

Courtesy Mrs. Maude Heller
THE WILLOWS STATION (SUTCLIFFE) AS IT APPEARED ABOUT 1900
Freight wagons, sometimes pulled by eighteen-horse teams, stopped here overnight. The tent provided eight single beds for weekend sports anglers.

Courtesy Dan Hellman, Pyramid Lake Resort, Nevada
JAMES SUTCLIFFE *(on the right)* WITH HIS WIFE AND SEVERAL FRIENDS AT THE WILLOWS STATION

bombing practice. Aircraft flying from the Fallon station launched unarmed torpedos at targets on the lake's surface and then retrieved the missiles by boat. A number of the big projectiles are known to have sunk, making it possible that a nine-thousand-year-old stone spearpoint, a hundred-year-old rifle ball, and a twentieth-century torpedo may be lying side by side in the depths of the desert lake.

Sea Serpents, Little Men, and Lost Treasure

Research of National Archive microfilms of the letter files of the Office of Indian Affairs often provides unexpected information.

Many northern Nevadans remember the reports (sometimes by reputed teetotalers) of sightings of the Pyramid sea serpent. The serpent has been generally considered to have had its origin in the imagination of the white man, but a letter written in 1870 indicated that the legend dates much farther back into the past.

In January of 1870, a Mr. H. Parker, of Carson City wrote Senator James W. Nye requesting that Pyramid Lake's Anaho Island be withdrawn from the reservation and used to raise "Cashmere goats." A petition addressed to the Secretary of the Interior and signed by Governor H. G. Blasdel and several other state officials, supported the request and pointed out that the Indians did not use the island because they held it in "superstitious dread."

The Acting Commissioner of the Office of Indian Affairs wrote Major Henry Douglas, Nevada Superintendent of Indian Affairs, for additional information,

Courtesy Martin Mifflin

EMERGING LIKE GIANT SEA MONSTERS, LARGE MASSES OF LAKE BOTTOM SEDIMENT CALLED "MUDLUMPS" MYSTERIOUSLY ROSE ABOVE THE SURFACE NEAR THE TRUCKEE DELTA IN 1967.

and Major Douglas, in turn, instructed Agent Le Bass to determine whether or not the Indians used the island. The report of Agent Le Bass, in part, follows:

Major Douglas
Carson City, Nevada

TRUCKEE RESERVATION
Jan 16, 1870

SIR

I duly received yours of the 10th instant and made inquiries of Winnemucca and other Indians if they had any superstitious ideas about the Pyramid Island. They say that their great grandfathers and grandmothers told them about seeing small Indians that would appear to them of a night. Their description of them was a large head and body and short legs, small feet. They also told of their ancestors seeing a large snake or serpent in the lake some two or three hundred feet long. They believe this but none of them have ever seen it. Some of the Indians visit the Island every spring for the purpose of gathering eggs and hatching young pelicans to eat. They often remain there for several days at a time. . . .

Agent Le Bass

The report of Agent Le Bass, in addition to clarifying the origin of the Sea Serpent legend, also explains why Anaho Island did not become a "Cashmere goat" farm.

On July 24, 1933, Nevada newspapers reported the death of Jimmie Shaw, one of Pyramid's oldest and very colorful Indians. According to the account, Shaw was a young man before he saw his first white person, and he claimed that he witnessed an early Indian attack on a group of Chinese traveling from California to the East. Apparently the Chinese were wealthy because their caravan was loaded with provisions and gold. The food was used by the Indians, but not realizing the value of the gold, they scattered some of it along the shores of Pyramid Lake and buried the remainder at the base of a mountain. Their neglect to mark the cache, and the many years of erosion which may have more deeply buried it, are given as the reasons why it has never been located. But the account claimed that from time to time gold coins had been found along the lake shore.

For a few hours during June of 1967 there was speculation that the Chinese gold had been discovered when a bulldozer, leveling land near the site of Fred Crosby's former trading post at Nixon, uncovered a cache that would have excited any treasure hunter. Indian boys and other members of the Pyramid Lake

FREMONT'S PYRAMID, WITH ANAHO ISLAND IN THE BACKGROUND

tribe reportedly picked up more than three thousand dollars' worth (face value) of gold coins which included valuable collectors' items such as a fifty-dollar gold piece and an 1814 Spanish doubloon. The Chinese caravan theory was dispelled when examination of the gold money revealed a mint date as late as 1917.

So the desert lake, not to be outdone by lakes in other parts of the world, has its lost treasure, its little people, and its serpent. And Nevadans probably can boast that their legend of the Pyramid Serpent had its origin much farther back into antiquity than that of a more famous Scottish monster.

CHAPTER III

The Desert Lake Today

IN 1932 a National Park Service official wrote, "The lake seems to live up to its claim of being the most beautiful desert lake in the United States."

A National Park Service investigation report in 1947 included, "It is no exaggeration to say that Pyramid is the most beautiful desert lake any member of the committee has yet seen—perhaps the most beautiful of its kind in North America."

Located about thirty miles northeast of Reno, Nevada, and accessible by either of two paved highways, Pyramid Lake is approximately twenty-five miles long, four to eleven miles wide, and more than three hundred feet deep. As the lake comes into view, its unique and strange beauty is almost startling. The colors of its water, the clean barrenness of its desert mountains, and its fantastic tufa formations glowing in the sunlight make it seem unreal. So often heard from Pyramid visitors that it may be a clue to the lake's attraction is the comment, "It seems like a place where time has stood still for thousands of years."

Color of Water

Its water has been described as constantly changing from shades of deep blue to green, and actually this does occur. Angle and intensity of the sunlight and suspended inorganic particles are factors, but plankton blooms during a certain time of the year bring the most spectacular transformations. Plankton, composed of algae (mostly one-celled plants) and tiny animals (largely crustaceans), floats freely in the lake and is an important part of the food chain. At times these small plants and animals increase in numbers until they become exceptionally dense in Pyramid's upper layer of water. Then when wind action disperses the plankton blanket and mixes it with deeper levels, the lake attains an unusual and beautiful turquoise hue. Unequal plankton density of the overturning water levels creates areas which differ in their shades of color.

Tufa

The tufa formations for which the lake is so well known are calcium carbonate deposits and are probably formed in at least five ways. According to the late Dr. Ira LaRivers, of the University of Nevada, the calcium carbonate is deposited: "(1) through the agency of algae; (2) by mechancial precipitation against shores and headlands, largely by wave action; (3) by precipitation from supersaturated waters entering the cold lake waters from hot springs (which are numerous in the Pyramid basin); (4) by precipitation in bottom muds through the action of hot, supersaturated water rising from below; and (5) by precipitation throughout the lake waters as they concentrate during periods of general dessication."

The Great Fishery

Although widely considered the most beautiful

THIS DESERT LAKE IS NOTED FOR ITS MANY UNUSUAL TUFA FORMATIONS

desert lake in North America, Pyramid's fishery actually brought it worldwide fame. A species of cutthroat
trout, technically classified as *Salmo clarki henshawi,*
grew to world-record size in the desert lake and attracted anglers from throughout the world.

For thousands of years the big Lahontan cutthroat,
named "Hoopagaih" by the Paiutes and called "redfish" by the whites, migrated up the Truckee River
to spawning areas. According to an early ichthyologist, John Otterbein Snyder, the redfish began moving upstream in October; and during winter months
literally crowded stretches of the river with their tre-
mendous numbers. And then in April, a smaller cutthroat, named "Tamaagaih" by the Indians and called
"Tommies" by white anglers, began their migration
run.

Before the white man, the cutthroat trout and the
cui-ui provided a bountiful food supply for Pyramid's
native Americans. Captured with spears, nets, traps,
and clubs as they ascended the river, many of the big
fish were split and hung on drying racks to preserve
them for seasons of less abundant food.

By the latter part of the nineteenth century the
whites were also heavily harvesting this great resource.
For instance, records show that in a six-months'
period, during the winter and spring of 1888 and
1889, one hundred tons of trout caught by commercial
fishermen were shipped by Wells, Fargo express and
railroad freight lines to many parts of the United
States. And in addition to the commercial catch, large
numbers of white sportsmen and Indians using
efficient steel gaff hooks instead of stone spearpoints

THE TRUCKEE RIVER, ISSUING FROM LAKE TAHOE, FLOWS NORTHEASTERLY
FOR ALMOST ONE HUNDRED MILES TO PYRAMID LAKE.

THE PYRAMID INDIANS DRY AND SMOKE CUI-UI FILLETS

were removing many more tons of fish from the lake and river.

Yet, even with this multiple harvest, there was no sign of a decrease in the supply of the Pyramid trout. With free access to upstream gravel beds, some of which were located in the Truckee's Sierra Nevada tributary streams, the great numbers of pink eggs carried by female cutthroat were ample to keep the species at a stable population. For years beyond the turn of the century, the supply of Pyramid fish was considered inexhaustible, and in 1912 the late Fred M. Crosby, who lived at Sutcliffe, Pyramid Lake, was shipping ten to fifteen tons of trout each week. Caught by his forty to fifty Indian fishermen, the cutthroat were sold in Tonopah, Goldfield, Manhat-

THE LATE FRANK LEONARD WAS ONE OF NEVADA'S FINEST OUT-
DOORSMEN, AND COMMERCIALLY FISHED PYRAMID LAKE IN THE
1890's.

tan, Rhyolite, and other mining towns and cities of Nevada.

But the process which brought extinction to the great Pyramid trout was already underway, and its agents were not the commercial fisherman, not the sport angler, not the Indian.

Dams built across the Truckee River partially blocked the spawning migration and, at times of low water, detoured returning Pyramid-bound fish from their river route into the irrigation ditches and cultivated fields of Truckee Meadow farmers. All of the Truckee's dams probably contributed to the decline of the trout population, but conservationists list one of them as the primary cause of extinction.

Located about twenty-five miles downriver from Reno, the Derby Dam was completed in 1905. The dam and its canal leading to the Lahontan Reservoir were part of the Bureau of Reclamation's Newlands Project, designed to combine the water from two separate watersheds for agricultural and electric power uses. Except during the periods of spring run-off or exceptionally high water, since 1905 much of the Truckee River's water has been diverted from its natural channel leading to Pyramid Lake and taken to another basin.

Some causes of the cutthroat's decline could have been controlled. Laws limiting the fisherman's harvest, fishways over dams, and screens at the mouths of irrigation ditches could have partially corrected the mistakes of the past. But the loss of the lake's water supply could not be balanced by artificial methods. The rapid drop in the lake's level exposed

THOUSANDS OF BIG CUTTHROAT TROUT ATTEMPTING TO JUMP THE
TRUCKEE RIVER DAMS WERE A COMMON SIGHT IN THE OLD DAYS

DERBY DAM DIVERTS WATER FROM THE TRUCKEE RIVER TO THE
CARSON RIVER DRAINAGE

Courtesy Nevada Fish and Game Commission
RENO HIGH SCHOOL BIOLOGY STUDENTS HELP FISHERIES PERSONNEL TO
TAG TROUT TO BE PLANTED IN PYRAMID LAKE
Tagging aids in the study of growth rates and survival
Courtesy Nevada Fish and Game Commission
A STATE FISH TRUCK BACKS TO THE EDGE OF THE WATER TO RELEASE
HATCHERY REARED CUTTHROAT TROUT INTO THE DESERT LAKE

STATE FISHERIES TECHNICIANS USE NETS AND SPECIALIZED EQUIPMENT TO
STUDY PYRAMID LAKE

BEST FISHING OCCURS BETWEEN OCTOBER AND THE FOLLOWING MARCH
WHEN THE WATER TEMPERATURES ARE COOL ENOUGH FOR THE TROUT
TO MOVE FROM DEEP WATER TO SHALLOWER AREAS

sandbars at the mouth of the Truckee which, together with the decreased flow of the lower river, made the spawning migration impossible.

It is probable that upstream water use by an expanding human population eventually would have decreased the lake's elevation, but it is believed that diversion of Truckee River water to the Carson River basin accelerated the process.

Perhaps it was during the twilight of their existence that the Pyramid trout obtained their most widespread fame. In December of 1925 a Paiute Indian, John Skimmerhorn, caught a forty-one-pound Lahontan cutthroat which still is listed as the world's record for its species. And undoubtedly larger fish were taken but not recorded. Fred Crosby reported that, in 1916, a cutthroat caught by an Indian weighed sixty-two pounds.

Famous men, including movie and sports celebrities, royalty from foreign countries, and U.S. President Herbert Hoover journeyed to Pyramid Lake during the 1920's and early thirties with the hope of landing a record trout. Paiute Indians guided these men, providing the boats and the knowledge necessary to catch the big fish as their numbers decreased.

And then the giant cutthroat of the desert lake were gone.

During the early 1940's incomplete studies led some biologists to conclude that the decrease in water volume had increased the concentration of dissolved salts until they were toxic to trout life. But a state fisheries technician conducted studies which reached a climax in August of 1948 when he submerged four

Courtesy Art Champagne
PRESIDENT HERBERT HOOVER, THE TWO LYMAN WILBURS, JR. AND SR.,
AND U.S. SUPREME COURT JUSTICE HARLAN FISKE STONE
Mr. Hoover caught the smallest trout of the week

cages, each containing eighty trout, to lake depths of 5, 10, 15, and 20 feet. The trout survived, and the simple experiment opened the door for an extensive restocking program which is still in progress. While Kokanee salmon and rainbow trout have been experimentally planted in the lake, studies indicate that the Lahontan cutthroat is better adapted to Pyramid's saline and alkaline environment.

The original cutthroat population of Pyramid was gone, but there was a possibility that the same strain might still exist in several other Nevada and California waters. Walker Lake, approximately seventy-five airline miles southeast of Pyramid, is also a rem-

Courtesy Art Champagne
CLARK GABLE WAS ONE OF THE MANY CELEBRITIES WHO CAME
TO FISH AT PYRAMID LAKE IN THE 1920's
AND EARLY 1930's

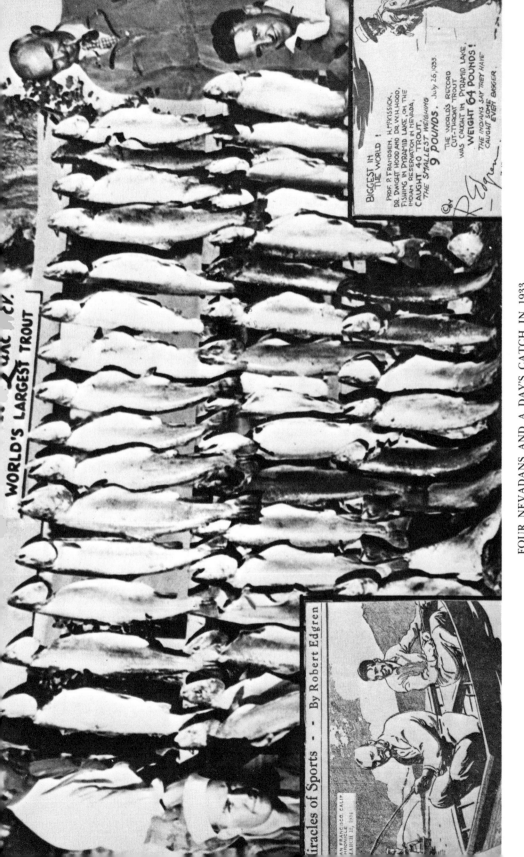

WORLD'S LARGEST TROUT

Miracles of Sports - - By Robert Edgren

SAN FRANCISCO, CALIF
CHRONICLE 17, 1931

FOUR NEVADANS AND A DAY'S CATCH IN 1933

nant of ancient Lake Lahontan; and its cutthroat
trout, despite several minor differences, are classified
as *Salmo clarki henshawi*. In the late 1940's, because
of conditions similar to Pyramid, the Lahontan cutthroat in Walker Lake were feared to be near extinction. But in 1949, a commercial carp fisherman, re-
trieving his large seine, found several of the big trout
fighting its meshes. Additional seinings by the state
fisheries personnel provided a total of thirty-nine of
the Walker cutthroat, which were transported to the
State's Verdi hatchery. The progeny of these original
fish now furnish part of the spawn required to restock
both Pyramid and Walker lakes.

And two other sources of what may be pure strain
Pyramid trout also provide eggs. During the 1920's
federal and state fisheries men established a spawn-
taking station at the mouth of the Truckee River,
and fertilized eggs from there were shipped to several
hatcheries. Although old records are vague, it is possible that Heenan Lake, near Markleville, California,
was stocked with Pyramid trout offspring; and, in cooperation with California fish and game officials, the
Nevada commission obtains spawn from this source.

Summit Lake, located on an isolated Indian reservation in northern Humboldt County, provides the
remaining eggs for Pyramid stocking. Again there is
not definite documentation, but Indians claim that
in 1928 a Paiute from Nixon transported a bucketful
of fertilized Pyramid trout spawn to Summit Lake to
start its trout population.

No one can be certain, but there is a possibility

A MORNING'S CATCH, ABOUT 1918, FROM THE TRUCKEE RIVER NEAR WADSWORTH

that descendants of the desert lake's original cutthroat are being returned to their native water.

Regardless of their exact inheritance, the planted trout are thriving in the alkaline and saline waters of Pyramid, and during recent years the lake has regained much of the prominence it enjoyed some fifty years ago as a big fish water. A twenty-seven-pound cutthroat, caught by Ralston Fillmore in 1978, is the largest recorded trout landed since the 1930's; but if some of the descriptions of fish which broke leaders are accurate, there may be another world record "Big Red" prowling the waters of the lake. The possibility of catching a trophy fish adds a certain extra to the sport and may be one reason for the number of anglers who travel long distances each year to fish the desert lake.

When waves are not "widow makers," the boat fishermen outnumber the shore casters. In the early days the favorite trolling lure was a large spoon-shaped attracter trailing a gut or wire leader with a hook imbedded in a fresh minnow. Today, all fish or other animal tissues are illegal, and anglers trail lures of various shapes, including the "daredevil" type which was also used in the old days.

According to one early day angler, very few people fished from shore during the Lake's heyday of the twenties and early thirties. But it is interesting to read famed ichthyologist, John Otterbein Snyder's, observations in 1911.

While studying the Lake and preparing his bulletin, "The Fishes of the Lahontan System of Nevada and Northeastern California,"* Snyder wrote that there

---

*Bulletin of the Bureau of Fisheries, Volume XXXV, 1915–16, Document No. 843, Issued September 28, 1917.

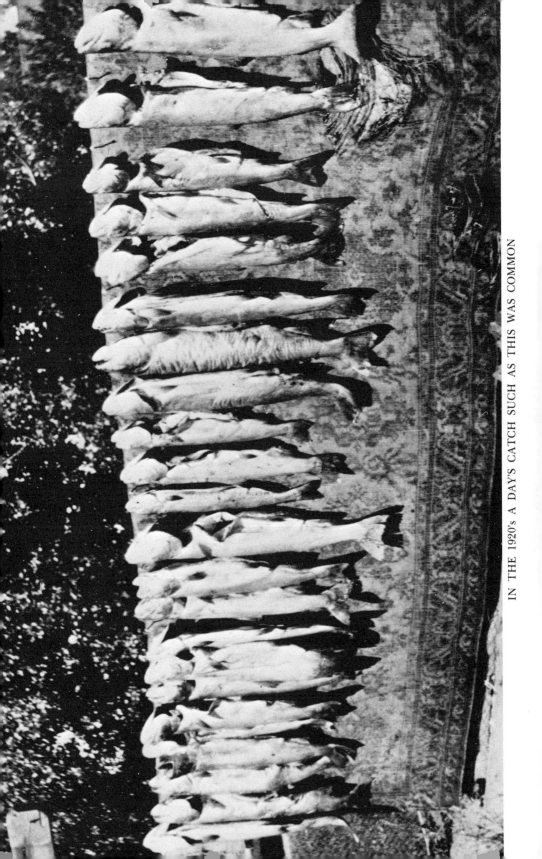

IN THE 1920's A DAY'S CATCH SUCH AS THIS WAS COMMON

IN 1948, THOMAS J. TRELEASE *(left)* PROVED THAT TROUT
COULD LIVE IN PYRAMID LAKE
Former Chief of Fisheries of the Nevada Fish and Game Commission, he first directed
the program of restocking the desert lake.

KAY JOHNSON, FORMER STATE FISHERIES TECHNICIAN, WITH A
CUTTHROAT TROUT.

were shore fishermen using, "a bamboo pole from 12 to 20 feet long and very stiff . . . supplied at regular intervals with large steel guide rings . . . a long, heavy line is passed outward through the rings and a lead from 2 to 8 ounces is attached. From the lead a 2 foot leader of wire or gut extends to a spinner with single, double, or triple hooks. The latter are used naked or baited."

The tackle did not include a reel, and Snyder explains, "The line is either coiled on the ground preparatory to a long cast or wound about the hand for a short one. A rapid side cast sends the line and its dangling tackle far out over the water."

Snyder apparently was an angler as well as a scientist, for after observing this crude method of fishing he decided to try his 5½ foot split bamboo rod with a reel filled with light braided line. He soon landed a 8¾ pound trout.

Apparently 1911 cutthroat responded to lures in much the same way they do today. Current shore casters who claim that trout follow and nudge their artificial baits will agree with Snyder's observation that, "the trout often followed the lure for a time before taking it. Sometimes the spoon was closely inspected or nosed and then abandoned."

Modern spinning tackle has simplified casting and provides the shore fisherman with a light rod which will throw a long line. Metal lures provide their own weight, but many spinning rod casters now use a woolyworm fly with a lead weight to carry out the monofilament line and sink it to the bottom. It is retrieved slowly enough to allow it to remain close to or scraping the bottom.

THE MONOFILAMENT LINE IS SPLICED TO THE THIRTY FEET OF
HEAVIER "SHOOTING HEAD" SINKING LINE. THE FLIES WERE TIED
BY EXPERIENCED PYRAMID ANGLER DR. STEPHEN CAMPBELL.
THE BOTTOM FLIES ARE TYPICAL WOOLYWORMS USED
BY MOST ANGLERS.

WITH THIRTY FEET OF "SHOOTING HEAD" SINKING LINE IN THE
AIR, THE BACK FALSE CAST PUTS A BEND IN THE LIGHT
GRAPHITE ROD.

But a new period in Pyramid Lake's angling history began when fly fishermen, using conventional fly rods, reels and lines, began catching fish. With an 8½ to 10½ foot fly rod (usually graphite) and a 30 foot "shooting head" sinking line attached to monofilament backing, the angler is able to cast a feather lure far enough to reach good fish areas.

Wading from shore as far as chest waders allow, the fly fisherman strips line off his reel until the required length of monofilament is floating on the surface in front of him or lies coiled in an open basket at his waist or chest. He then false casts until the thirty feet of heavier sinking line is in the air and, with a final cast, sends it shooting out over the water dragging the light monofilament behind. The line and fly are allowed to sink and then the fly is retrieved slowly enough for it to remain near the lake bed.

This brief description of the currently most widely used method of fly fishing from shore is written for those who are making their first trip to the lake. More detailed information can be obtained at the Pyramid Lake Store at the fish checking station on the Pyramid Lake highway (33) one mile before the lake comes into view, and at Crosby Lodge at Sutcliffe. The Pyramid Lake Ranger Station at Sutcliffe will also provide fishing permits and regulations.

An excellent attitude toward sport fishing is noticeable among many of the lake's experienced anglers. It is not unusual to see some fishermen regularly releasing, without injury, legal size and much larger trout, satisfied with just the sport of landing the big ones. Because of the heavy fishing pressure on the lake, it is encouraging to see the increasing number of these sport anglers. But Pyramid trout are fine eating, and those who enjoy them should not hesitate to keep (within the legal limit) what they need for fish dinners.

Shore casting begins when the water cools in the late fall, and the larger fish move in. During mid-winter days, when lines freeze in the guides, there are some non-fishermen who question the sanity of the many casters standing chest deep in the cold water. Proper clothing under the wading gear is essential.

Shore fishing for legal size fish usually ends in early spring when the shallows warm, and the large trout return to deep water.

Fish growth in the lake is remarkably rapid. The late Dr. Ira LaRivers, of the University of Nevada, summed up his studies of the lake's food conditions by saying, "Pyramid is literally a culture medium for all organisms in the food chain — temperatures are warm, nutrients are plentiful, and fish growth rapid — and so is capable of producing the maximum yields of game fish that could possibly be expected anywhere."

Pyramid Lake Fisheries has developed two cutthroat trout hatcheries, a cui-ui fish hatchery, and a system of rearing tanks and raceways. According to Fisheries Director, Paul Wagner, the Dunn Hatchery, located near Sutcliffe, has been averaging 600,000 trout planted annually. The Numana Hatchery, near the Truckee River between Nixon and Wadsworth, began operation in 1981, and in 1986 will also plant

600,000 cutthroat. The Lahontan National Fish Hatchery, in Douglas County, annually provides 500,000 six inch trout, making an approximate total yearly plant of 1,700,000 cutthroat in Pyramid Lake.

The raceway and brood tank system, completed in 1981, uses Pyramid Lake water to acclimate the fish to their future environment and is designed to rear fingerling trout to a size which will bring a higher rate of survival when they are released into the lake. A fishway, designed to allow fish to bypass the delta at the mouth of the Truckee River, ascend the Marble Bluff Dam, and migrate upstream, was built in 1976. Up until 1983, the number of cutthroat using the fishway was limited. However, higher water and a method of lifting the fish over the dam has allowed greater planting of fingerlings above the dam. It is believed that the fishway eventually will become a significant passage for fish instinctively returning to the Truckee River for spawning.

Currently, during the spring spawning season, mature cutthroat attempt to return to where they were reared, ascending the stream which runs from the raceway and brood tanks system to the lake. There technicians strip the eggs from the females, fertilize the eggs with the sperm of the male fish, and return the spawned fish to the lake.

During 1986 this operation provided 3,200,000 fertilized eggs for the two hatcheries and 1,500,000 for the Lahontan National Fish Hatchery.

The cui-ui sucker (Chasmistes cujus) is endemic to the lake and is a valuable food fish. Although commonly thought also to live in a lake in Asia, the cui-ui

THE CUI-UI FISH, A MEMBER OF THE SUCKER FAMILY WEIGHTS UP TO NINE POUNDS AND IS FOUND ONLY IN PYRAMID LAKE

CUI-UI WERE CAUGHT WITH SNAG HOOKS AS THEY LIE OFF THE SANDBAR AT THE MOUTH OF THE TRUCKEE RIVER

"ABE" AND SUE ABRAHAMS OWNED AND OPERATED THE STORE AT NIXON FOR
MANY YEARS.

Courtesy Nevada Fish and Game Commission

DR. IRA LaRIVERS, OF THE UNIVERSITY OF NEVADA, EXAMINES DEAD CUI-UI
LEFT STRANDED ON A GRAVEL BAR NEAR THE MOUTH
OF THE TRUCKEE RIVER

is found only in Pyramid. Rather close relatives are known to live in Klamath Lake and Utah Lake, both of which are remnants of Pleistocene lakes. Because the cui-ui is an endangered species, fishing for them is currently illegal.

During summer months when trout fishing from shore is the least productive, the Sacramento Perch once provided anglers with good sport. A native to California, the Sacramento Perch once provided anglers with good sport. A native to California, the Sacramento Perch is thought to have become established in the Truckee River drainage in 1889. While for many years it had been known that a large population of these fish existed in Pyramid Lake, until the 1950's, most efforts to catch them on sporting tackle were unsuccessful. When it was discovered that the perch would strike an artificial lure (such as a nymph or fly) if it was slowly dragged along the bottom to imitate a crawling insect, creel limits became common. Although some Sacramento Perch are known to still live in the lake, no limit catches have been reported in recent years.

Once known to anglers throughout the world, the desert lake's cutthroat trout are again bringing it fame among those who enjoy the sport of fishing with rod and reel.

Water Sports

In addition to angling, the desert lake offers many other types of recreation to its visitors. Its more than seventy miles of sandy beaches and warm surface waters are ideal for water skiing, swimming and boating. Boating offers an opportunity to explore the interesting shorelines of the ancient lake, but caution is advisable. At one moment the surface of the desert lake may be calm, but a sudden wind can transform it into ocean-like waves which only a boat with ample freeboard and a competent pilot can stay afloat. Allen Crosby at Sutcliffe has made over forty rescues of boats in trouble, gaining the widespread respect of Pyramid boatmen and an award from the Western States Boating Law Administrators Association.

Plants and Animals

Plant life of the lake's basin is typical of a cold desert flora, with sagebrush, rabbit brush, and shad scale the most common of the larger perennial plants. Many species of smaller annuals compete for the basin's available moisture.

Animals include interesting species of reptiles, mammals, arachnids, and birds.

Reptiles (such as the beautiful collared lizard, the interesting and docile horned lizard, and the speedy whip-tailed, swift, and leopard lizards) are most commonly seen by visitors. Fortunately, only one species of poisonous snake, the Great Basin rattlesnake, is found in northern Nevada.

Mammals of the area include one of the most interesting and intelligent carnivores in North America, the coyote. This little desert wolf, so much resembling a domestic dog, is often seen retreating up a hillside, and his barking at night is a pleasant sound to those who enjoy Nevada deserts. Mule deer are found in both the Virginia Range on the west and the Lake Range to the east. Other common mammals

AT SUTCLIFFE, TWO ESTABLISHMENTS OFFER SERVICES
TO PYRAMID LAKE VISITORS
This is now named the Sutcliffe Inn

CROSBY LODGE AT SUTCLIFFE

TWO FORMER OLD-TIMERS OF THE PYRAMID LAKE AREA
Fred Crosby *(left)* first visited the lake in 1893. William W. Cogswell was
a Nevada rancher and miner.

include the black-tailed jackrabbit, the cottontail rabbit, the bobcat, and several species of rodents. The little antelope ground squirrel can be readily recognized by its white tail curled up and over its back. The kangaroo rat, a nocturnal animal, can often be seen in the evening.

One arachnid, commonly called the tarantula, deserves mention. Although a very interesting spider, superstition and its large size have caused it to be feared by many humans. Similar to other spiders, it does have poison glands for paralyzing its prey, but its toxin is not generally considered dangerous to adult humans, and naturalists have found that it is difficult, often impossible, to coax one of the big spiders to bite man. Tarantulas, though common in the basin, are largely nocturnal. During a certain time of year, males may be seen crossing the highway.

Although the desert lake offers a resting area to many species of migratory waterfowl, it is best known for its pelicans. Anaho Island is the site of probably the largest of the seven white pelican nesting colonies in North America. In July of 1965, United States Fish and Wildlife Service personnel estimated a total of 7,500 young and adult white pelicans which were sharing the island's approximately 750 acres* with 1,500 double-breasted cormorants, 4,500 California gulls, 150 Caspian terns, and 200 great blue herons.

In 1913 President Woodrow Wilson declared Anaho Island a national wildlife refuge, and since then visitors have not been allowed to land there except under an official permit. To those who have visited Anaho, the screeching of its crowded bird life,

---

* See W. Verne Woodbury, "The History and Present Status of the Biota of Anaho Island, Pyramid Lake, Nevada" (Master's thesis, University of Nevada, 1966).

the gulls wheeling overhead, and the thousands of nests make it seem like an ocean island.

BEYOND THE PYRAMID, ANAHO ISLAND

IN JULY OF 1965 THERE WERE MORE THAN SEVEN THOUSAND
WHITE PELICANS ON ANAHO ISLAND

WHITE PELICANS FEEDING AT THE MOUTH OF THE TRUCKEE RIVER

PELICANS HAVE BEEN ACCUSED OF CATCHING PYRAMID GAME FISH
Studies of regurgitated stomach contents indicate they feed almost entirely on
chubs and other rough fish.

BOAT AND ANGLERS ARE DWARFED BY THE DESERT LAKE'S PYRAMID
In July of 1967, it stood 365 feet above the surface.

CHAPTER IV

The Future

ANY STEADY DECREASE in the depth of Pyramid Lake is a matter of concern to many Nevadans, and to others interested in the desert lake. Using recorded elevations provided by the late H. Claude Dukes, Federal Court Watermaster for the Truckee River, and the U.S. Geologic Survey, variations during the past are compiled below. Changes are listed, in most instances, for five year periods, the exceptions falling between 1867 and 1922 when measurements were not made every year. Partially because early elevations were not always measured at the same time of the year, a total of the listed gains and losses would be somewhat inaccurate.

YEARS	PERIOD OF YEARS	APPROXIMATE DECREASE IN ELEVATION (Feet)	APPROXIMATE INCREASE IN ELEVATION (Feet)
1867 - 1871	4		9
1871 - 1882	11	19	
1882 - 1889	7	7	
1889 - 1890	1		16
1890 - 1904	14	13	
1904 - 1909	5		7
1909 - 1914	5	3	
1914 - 1917	3	5	
1917 - 1922	5	5	
1922 - 1927	5	9	
1927 - 1932	5	15	
1932 - 1937	5	14	
1937 - 1942	5		1
1942 - 1947	5	6	

YEARS	PERIOD OF YEARS	APPROXIMATE DECREASE IN ELEVATION (Feet)	APPROXIMATE INCREASE IN ELEVATION (Feet)
1947 - 1952	5	3	
1952 - 1957	5	7	
1957 - 1962	5	12	
1962 - 1966	5	5	
1967 - 1972	5		6
1972 - 1979	7	6	
1979 - 1986	7		29.4

According to United States Geological Survey publications and certain authorities, the elevation of Pyramid Lake in 1867, established by means of photograph comparisons was approximately 3,876 feet above sea level.† However, Hardman and Venstrom interpolated, from King, the 1867 elevation at 3,867 feet.‡

In September of 1986, after exceptionally heavy precipitation, the U.S. Geological Survey measured the lake's surface elevation at 3,816.7 feet above sea level.* If the 3,876-foot figure is used for 1867, Pyramid's depth has decreased approximately 59 feet in 119 years. Use of the Hardman-Venstrom elevation indicates the lake has lowered about 50 feet in the same time period.

According to S. T. Harding,§ the area of Pyramid

---

† Clarence King, *Geological Exploration of the Fortieth Parallel* (Vol. I; Washington, 1870). Also I. C. Russell, *Geological History of Lake Lahontan* ("U.S. Geological Survey, Monograph 11"). Adjusted to datum of 1929 through supplementary datum of 1956.

‡ See George Hardman and Cruz Venstrom, "A One Hundred Year Record of Truckee River Runoff Estimated from Changes in Levels and Volumes of Pyramid and Winnemucca Lakes,"*American Geophysical Union Transactions* (1941).

* On June 30, 1987, the level had dropped to 3,815.3, a decrease of 1.4 feet.

§ S. T. Harding, "Evaporation from Pyramid and Winnemucca Lakes," *Journal of the Irrigation and Drainage Division, Proceedings of the American Society of Civil Engineers,* March, 1962.

PYRAMID LAKE SURFACE ELEVATIONS

1871 to 1986

Courtesy Mrs. Maude Heller
IN THE EARLY 1900's THE TUFA ROCKS AT SUTCLIFFE WERE ON
THE EDGE OF THE LAKE

IN 1966 THE LEVEL OF THE LAKE WAS FAR BELOW THE TUFA
ROCKS AT SUTCLIFFE

Lake varied from 135,000 acres in 1927 to 115,000 acres in 1960. Due to the increase in water flowing into the lake between 1982 and 1986, it now covers the same 115,000 acres that it did in 1960. The only outlet to the lake is evaporation, which is computed at approximately four feet annually.

It is interesting to note that during high water periods Pyramid's sister lake, Winnemucca, was largely fed by overflow from Pyramid through a slough connecting the two lakes; and that, at the time of its first records prior to 1850, it was dry, or nearly so. It is thought that the Truckee River flood of 1862 greatly increased the depth of the water in the Winnemucca Lake basin, which continued to gain until it measured approximately eighty feet in 1882. A downward trend from 1905 resulted in the lake again becoming dry in 1939.

Pyramid Lake water contains approximately 5,000 parts per million dissolved solids of which, in 1986, 68 percent was sodium chloride. Cutthroat trout are known to tolerate considerably larger amounts of this salt.

The pH (alkalinity) of the lake in 1986 was 9.1, which compares to a range of 6.5 to 8.5 for most lakes. Fortunately, during recent years the pH seems to be remaining fairly constant and is tolerated by the lake's present fish population.

Based on its present rate of desiccation, it has been estimated that Pyramid Lake will remain suitable for fish life for seventy-five to one hundred years. An accurate estimate is difficult. Winters of heavy precipitation will lengthen the period; drought and man's additional uses of Truckee River water will shorten it.

The future of North America's most beautiful desert lake will be, as it has been for seventy thousand years, controlled by its water supply.

Fishing and water sports currently bring many people to Pyramid, but to those who love the desert lake it is a special place. They know its friendly beauty as the morning sun paints its mountains with pinks and reds, and they feel its strength when storm clouds sweep in from the west and waves break white against tufa domes. And at a certain time of the year,* if they are fortunate, they may see something unusual.

As the sun drops behind the Virginia Range, its last shaft of light, funneled through a mountain pass and low clouds, strikes only a triangular shaped rock so that it stands out alone against its dark background. It is beautiful but strange; and as one stands watching it he may wonder if others — perhaps an early Asian migrant or the great war chief, Numaga — may have paused to watch the sun's rays glow and then fade on an odd-shaped mass of stone — the pyramid of the desert lake.

Courtesy
Thomas R. C. Wilson, II
FROM BENEATH STORM
CLOUDS, THE LAST OF
THE DAY'S SUNLIGHT
STRIKES THE
FANTASTICALLY
BEAUTIFUL NEEDLES

---

* The writer watched this occur on the evening of November 6, 1966.

Bibliography

Angel, Myron (ed.). *History of Nevada.* ("Deluxe Facsimile Reproduction Series.") Oakland, Calif.: Thompson and West, 1881. Reprint; Berkeley, Calif.: Howell-North Books, 1958.

Antevs, Ernst. "Climatic Changes and Pre-White Man in the Great Basin with Emphasis on Glacial and Post Glacial Times," *Utah University Bulletin,* Vol. XXXVIII, No. 20 (1948).

Ashbaugh, Don. *Nevada's Turbulent Yesterdays.* Los Angeles: Westernlore Publishers, 1963.

Atwater, Jane. "Legendary Lake of the Paiutes," *Desert Magazine,* November, 1954.

Bancroft, Hubert Howe. *History of Nevada, Colorado, and Wyoming, 1540-1888.* San Francisco: San Francisco History Club, Publishers, 1889.

Broecker, Wallace S., and Kaufman, Aaron. "Radiocarbon Chronology of Lake Lahontan and Lake Bonneville II, Great Basin," *Bulletin of the Geological Society of America,* Vol. LXXVI (1965).

————and Orr, Phil C. "Radiocarbon Chronology of Lake Lahontan and Lake Bonneville," *Bulletin of the Geological Society of America,* Vol. LXIX (1958).

Bruce, Irene. "Legend of Pyramid Lake," *Catholic World,* February, 1942.

Cline, Gloria Griffen. *Exploring the Great Basin.* Norman, Okla.: University of Oklahoma Press, 1963.

Davis, Sam P. (ed.). *The History of Nevada.* 2 vols.; Reno, Nev., and Los Angeles, Calif.: Elms Publishing Company, 1913.

Fairbanks, H. W. "Pyramid Lake," *Popular Science,* March 1901.

Fairfield, Asa Merrill. *Fairfield's Pioneer History of Lassen*

County, California. San Francisco: published for the author by H. S. Crocker Company (1916).

Frémont, Brev. Capt. John Charles. *Report of the Exploring Expedition to the Rocky Mountains in the Year 1842 and to Oregon and North California in the years 1843-'44.* U.S. Senate, 28th Cong., 2nd Sess., Exec. Doc. 174. Washington D.C.: Gales and Seton, Printers, 1845.

Gromme, Owen J. "A Sojourn Among the Wildfowl of Pyramid Lake," *Yearbook of the Public Museum of Milwaukee* (1930).

Harding, S. T. "Evaporation from Pyramid and Winnemucca Lakes," *Journal of the Irrigation and Drainage Division, Proceedings of the American Society of Civil Engineers,* March, 1962.

Hardman, George, and Venstrom, Cruz. "A One Hundred Year Record of Truckee River Runoff Estimated from Changes in Levels and Volumes of Pyramid and Winnemucca Lakes," *American Geophysical Union Transactions* (1941).

Heizer, Robert F. *Archaeological Radiocarbon Dates from California and Nevada.* ("The University of California Archaeological Survey Reports," No. 44, Part 1, 1958.)

———and Baumhoff, Martin A. *Prehistoric Rock Art of Nevada and Eastern California.* Berkeley, Calif.: University of California Press, 1962.

Hinkle, George Henry, and Hinkle, Bliss M. *Sierra-Nevada Lakes* ("American Lakes Series.") Indianapolis, Ind.: The Bobbs-Merrill Company, Inc., 1949.

Houghton, Samuel G. "The Truckee River Story," *Nevada Highways and Parks Magazine,* Spring, 1966.

Jennings, Jesse D., and Norbeck, Edward. "Great Basin Prehistory: A Review," *American Antiquity,* XXI (1955) No. 1, 1-11.

Johnson, Frank. "The Tribe That Failed Its Destiny," *Nevada State Journal,* November 6, 1966.

Jones, J. Claude. *Geologic History of Lake Lahontan.* Reno, Nev.: University of Nevada.

Kappler, Charles J. (ed.). *Indian Affairs, Laws and Treaties. Compiled to December 1, 1902.* Compiled and edited by Charles J. Kappler, clerk of the Senate Committee on

Indian Affairs. Washington: Government Printing Office, 1904.

King, Clarence. *Geological Exploration of the Fortieth Parallel.* ("U.S. Army Engineers, Professional Paper No. 18.") Vol. I; Washington: Government Printing Office, 1870.

LaRivers, Ira. *Fish and Fisheries of Nevada.* Carson City, Nev.: Nevada State Fish and Game Commission, 1962.

Liebling, Abbott Joseph. "The Lakes of the Cui-ui Eaters," *New Yorker,* January 1-22, 1955.

Lillard, Richard G. *Desert Challenge: An Interpretation of Nevada.* New York: Alfred A. Knopf, 1942.

Lincoln, Frances C. *Mining Districts and Mineral Resources of Nevada.* Reno, Nev.: Newsletter Publishing Company, 1923.

Lomas, Marie. "Lake of Doom," *Nature Magazine,* June 1942.

————. "Sphinx of Pyramid Lake," *Desert Magazine,* February, 1939.

Loud, Llewellyn L., and Harrington, Mark R. "Lovelock Cave," *American Archaeology and Ethnology,* Vol. XXV. Berkeley, Calif.: University of California Press, 1929.

Mack, Effie Mona. *Nevada, a History of the State from the Earliest Times through the Civil War.* Glendale, Calif.: The Arthur H. Clark Company, 1936.

————and Sawyer, Byrd Wall. *Our State: Nevada.* Caldwell, Idaho: The Caxton Printers, Ltd., 1940.

————. *Here Is Nevada.* Sparks, Nev.: Western Printing and Publishing Company, 1965.

McCulloch, Frank. "How the Great Spearhead Came to Pyramid Lake," *Nevada Magazine,* August, 1947.

Miller, William Charles. "The Pyramid Lake Indian War of 1860," *Nevada Historical Society Quarterly,* September-November, 1957.

Morrison, R. B. *Lake Lahontan: Geology of the Southern Carson Desert, Nevada.* ("U.S. Geological Survey, Professional Paper 401.") Washington, D.C., 1964.

————. *Lake Lahontan Stratigraphy and History in the Carson Desert (Fallon) Area, Nevada.* ("U.S. Geological Survey, Professional Paper 424-D.") Washington, D.C., 1961.

————and Frye, John C. *Correlation of the Middle and Late Quaternary Successions of the Lake Lahontan, Lake Bonneville, Rocky Mountain (Wasatch Range), Southern Great Plains and Eastern Midwest Areas.* ("Nevada Bureau of Mines Report No. 9.") Carson City, Nev.

Myrick, David F. *Railroads of Nevada and Eastern California.* 2 vols.; Berkeley, Calif.: Howell-North Books, 1962-63.

National Archives Microcopies. Letters Received by the Office of Indian Affairs, Nevada Superintendency, 1861-1880.

————. Letters Received by the Office of Indian Affairs, Utah Superintendency, 1859-1860.

National Geographic Society (Washington, D.C.). *Indians of the Americas.* ("Story of Man Library.") Washington, D.C., 1955.

Nevada Highways and Parks Magazine. "Pyramid Lake," No. 2, 1957.

————. "Pyramid, a Strange Desert Lake," January-April, 1954.

Nevada State Fish and Game Commission. "Pyramid Lake Fisheries Management Report, June, 1958."

Newcomer, E. J. "Pyramid Lake," *Overland Monthly,* October, 1914.

Orr, Phil C. "Pleistocene Man in Fishbone Cave, Pershing County, Nevada." Nevada State Museum, *Bulletin No. 2,* 1956.

————. "Preliminary Excavations of Pershing County Caves." Nevada State Museum, *Bulletin No. 1,* 1952.

Riddell, Francis A. "Honey Lake Paiute Ethnography." Nevada State Museum, *Anthropological Paper No. 4.*

Russell, I. C. *Geological History of Lake Lahontan, a Quaternary Lake of Northwestern Nevada.* ("U.S. Geological Survey, Monograph 11.") Washington, 1885.

Sacramento Bee. Reports on Pyramid Lake War, May-June, 1860.

Sacramento Union. Reports on Pyramid Lake War, May-June, 1860.

Sanford, John. "Pyramid Lake's Level is Down Nearly 100 Feet Since Discovery," *Reno Evening Gazette,* September 10, 1966.

Shutler, Richard. "Correlation of Beach Terraces with Climatic Cycles of Pluvial Lake Lahontan, Nevada," *Annals of the New York Academy of Sciences,* Vol. XCV, Art. 1, 1961.

Stewart, O. C. "Culture Element Distributions, XIV: Northern Paiute," *Anthropological Records,* Vol. IV. Berkeley, Calif.; University of California Press, 1940-41.

Stone, Margaret. "Pelicans of Pyramid," *Desert Magazine,* June, 1943.

Sunset. "Look What Is Just a Few Minutes from Reno," June, 1966.

————. "Nevada's Vast Desert Lake," November, 1955.

Trelease, Thomas J. "Death of a Lake," *Field and Stream,* February, 1952.

Tuohy, Donald R. "Nevada's Prehistoric Heritage," Nevada State Museum Popular Series, No. 1, 1965.

Underhill, Ruth. *The Northern Paiute Indians of California and Nevada.* Lawrence, Kan.: Haskell Institute, 1941.

U.S. Senate. 36th Cong., 1st Sess., 1859-60. I, 730.

Wheat, Margaret M. *Notes on Paviotso Material Culture.* Nevada State Museum Anthropological Papers, No. 1.

Wheeler, Sessions S. *Paiute.* Caldwell, Idaho: The Caxton Printers, Ltd., 1965.

Wren, Thomas (ed.). *A History of the State of Nevada, Its Resources and People.* Chicago: Lewis Historical Publishing Company, 1904.

Wright, William. *The Big Bonanza; An Authentic Account of the Discovery, History, and Working of the World-Renowned Comstock Lode of Nevada.* ("Western Americana.") New York: Alfred A. Knopf, 1947.

Woodbury, W. Verne. "The History and Present Status of the Biota of Anaho Island, Pyramid Lake, Nevada." Unpublished Master's thesis, University of Nevada, 1966.

ABOUT THE AUTHOR

Sessions S. "Buck" Wheeler, kneeling on a tufa dome above Pyramid Lake, is a widely recognized outdoorsman, conservationist, teacher and western writer whose successful historical novel and desert nonfiction books have received national and international attention.

For this sixth printing of THE DESERT LAKE, he has rewritten the last two chapters to provide information on fly fishing for Pyramid's large cutthroat trout and to update the lake's rise in surface elevation. The current Indian fish stocking program and an interesting account of shore fishing in 1911 are also included.

"Wheeler covers the entire scene — archaeology, hydrogeography, anthropology, fauna and flora and ichthyology, and the bitter warfare that developed inevitably between native and white man.

"It is a fascinating story, so close to our own backyard."
— *Sacramento Union*

"The book with heavy paper cover, will make interesting reading for the fisherman, the historian, the geologist, the scenery seeker."
— Medford (Oregon) *Mail-Tribune*

"This story of Pyramid Lake contains more than 70 excellent illustrations. Geology, archeology, history, biology, recreation, present situation, and future of Pyramid Lake are accurately and ably discussed and illustrated by a man who thoroughly knows the subject and has a delightful writing style.
— The Nevada Archeological Survey *Reporter*

The book tells in sweeping style the story of Nevada's famous Pyramid Lake . . . *The Desert Lake* is an interesting, informative popular study. . . . One leaves this book with a deep desire to pay the lake a visit.
— Lonnie J. White, Professor of History, Memphis State University, Memphis, Tennessee

The CAXTON PRINTERS, Ltd.
CALDWELL, IDAHO